Creative Crafts
of the
World

Marilyn Romatka

Taproot Folk Arts

Published by
Taproot Folkarts
Bellevue, WA 98006
www.taprootfolkarts.com

© 2012 Marilyn Romatka

All rights reserved. Except for brief excerpts for review or use in classroom teaching, this book may not be reproduced in part or in whole by electronic means or otherwise without written permission of the publisher. All rights reserved.

Studio photography by Rainer Romatka. Snapshots by Marilyn Romatka. Additional picture by Moses Kinayia. Copyright held by the respective owners.

Graphics in Paper Stars, Twining and Dreamcatcher by Kevin E. Cain. Additional graphics by Rainer Romatka.

The author advises caution when using sharp knives, fancy glues, hot dye-pots (etc.) with children and is not responsible for any injuries resulting from following the instructions in this book. Furthermore the copyright holders and/or other parties provide the instructions in the book 'as is' without warranty of any kind, expressed or implied, including, but not limited to, the **implied warranties of merchantability and fitness for a particular purpose**.

The following are all registered trade marks: Michael's, JoAnn, Ben Franklin, Sharpie markers, Tacky Glue, Q-tips, GUM floss threaders, Scotch tape, E6000 glue, Superglue, Elmer's glue, Murphy's Oil Soap, Popsicle, Lamb's Pride yarn, X-Acto knives, Tulip brand fabric paint, Kinko's, Western Family, Pyrex

Published 2012

Manufactured in the United States of America

ISBN-13: 978-0-9853538-0-3
ISBN-10: 0985353805
Library of Congress Catalog Number: 2012906137

This book is dedicated to

my
Mom and Dad

who both taught me from an early age
the *joy* that comes from making something
with your own hands

Table of Contents

Introduction 8

Aboriginal Dot Painting 10

Viking Knitting 16

Huichol Beading......................................26

Natural Dyes 30

Weaving 42

Baumschmuck 50

Paper Stars...56

Block Printing...64

Pysanky 72

Dream Catcher 82

Wet Felting.............................88

Twining 96

Maasai Beading 104

Bow Loom Weaving 110

Dragon Boats 118

For your Inspiration.............126
Appendix A Dot Paint 131
Appendix B Pysanky 136
Appendix C Resources......138

INTRODUCTION

Years ago, it started with a young llama. My husband surprised me with a charming cria for Christmas to be our pack animal while hiking in the mountains. The llama needed to be shorn so as not to overheat on the trail, and it didn't take long before I had bags full of the stuff.

A friend commented that I should learn to spin. "People still do that?" I asked.

Well, it turns out they *do*. I learned to spin, then knit, then weave. It gave me incredible pleasure to watch the fiber go through all the steps: shearing, washing, carding, spinning, plying, knitting. I did it all – from the llama's back to a garment on *my* back. It was a whole, wholesome, living undertaking, so much different from walking into a department store and purchasing something made by machines in mass production. I was hooked.

I had been quilting since I was in middle school, but this *making cloth* thing was a revelation. Thus began the next level of my love-affair with articles made by the human hand. I dabbled in techniques from different countries, always drawn to folk art from an early age. I would show up at Spinner's Guild weaving on the bow loom, and before long people started asking me to teach them the different techniques I had accumulated. My teaching style, because of my sequential science (biochemistry) background, turned out to be a good one they tell me – clear and 'chunked-down' into steps that made sense. Soon after, people started asking me to teach their children.

All this led to teaching weekly at the local home school co-operative, where I started actively researching other ethnic techniques in order to offer the students a well-rounded folk art expe-

rience. I loved learning how peoples from all over the world decorated the everyday things around them, how they made the useful things in their lives beautiful! But even more fun than the learning was the *teaching*. There is no greater thrill than watching a young student sitting at the spinning wheel, working for a couple of class-sessions at the new skill of pumping the treadle at the same time as drafting the fuzzy, wayward fibers of their roving, and actually **seeing** the light bulb go on when it 'clicks' for them and they go from being a normal suburban kid to a *spinner* – now connected to untold generations before them.

This is why I have a passion for passing traditional skills on to the next generation. Something happens to a child at that point, when they acquire a skill so very basic to human development. I have seen the same thing in the basketry unit: when they master a skill this old, they are more *grounded*. They can do something *real*, something more than the latest 'fad'.

This is the relevance of folk art in the modern, electronic era. It grounds us in the past, it connects us to the generations that came before us. It opens our eyes (and more importantly the young students' eyes) to the point of view of other peoples in other countries and in other times. Teaching them about another country's art opens up opportunities to start discussions on geography, history, sociology, and more. Working on an ethnic craft provides the time to talk about all these while young hands are busy creating.

This book is meant to be a catalyst for you and whatever group of children has been entrusted to you, be it in a classroom, a birthday party, or just a morning at grandma's for crafting. Teach them well. Have fun.

Marilyn

P.S. A comment on costumes: when teaching kids, I always wear folk clothing. This gives us even one more opening to discuss folk culture. I have seen some kids really light up when we discuss other cultures and their specific styles and skills for clothing themselves. With elementary kids, I even have a dress-up day with Guatemalan clothing, their size! What better way to open their eyes to the idea that there are other kids 'out there' whose lives are different from theirs? I also try to play culture-appropriate music during a crafting session. This catches the music lovers in the same way.

Aboriginal Dot Painting

This is truly one of the most charming folk art styles available to us; a technique simple to execute, yet one that produces an emotionally moving painting. Traditionally done on bark, contemporary versions go well on paper or even other surfaces. Furniture is an especially nice venue for dot painting – a great way to let a child personalize their own room.

History

From Northern Queensland with its X-ray style and crosshatching, to the dots of the central deserts, Aboriginal artists produce stunningly beautiful paintings. They have used the same symbols from the time of the cave painting to today. The symbols and the stories they tell have deep cultural significance to the clans. The paintings replay and celebrate the time of the Dreaming when, they believe, the ancestors roamed the barren land and shaped the landscape, sky, animals and the rules for the earth.

We in the western world can appreciate the beauty of the paintings even without understanding the full significance these paintings and symbols hold in the Australian Aboriginal culture.

New Vocabulary

<u>Australian Aborigines</u>: Natives of Australia

<u>Art docent</u>: A person specifically teaching art in a classroom

Class Preparation

I get my dot painting paper at the local craft shop in their scrap-booking section. I choose the 12 x 12 inch size because it gives the young artists more space to "weave their dreams" on. Ideally I like to get paper that looks like bark or wood to keep the project as close to the authentic folk art as possible. Darker paper ends up looking nicer.

The paints I use are acrylic paints, also purchased at the local craft shop. The Aboriginals use mostly earth tones and vibrant primary colors. Of course, you are free to use grey tones or pastels to your own taste, depending on how authentic you wish your group's lesson to be.

Use washed milk jug tops as paint wells – this gives you "just the right amount" of

Materials

- Paper 12 x 12 inch
- Acrylic paint
- Q-tips
- Scissors
- Milk caps for paint wells
- Stencils (see reference pages)
- Sharpie pens of many colors
- Practice paper
- Table drapes

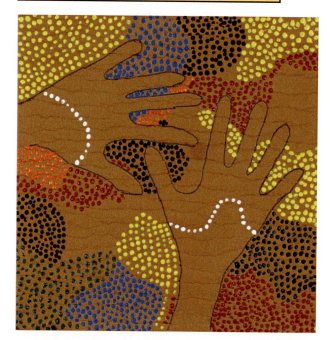

Creative Crafts of the World — Aboriginal Dot Painting

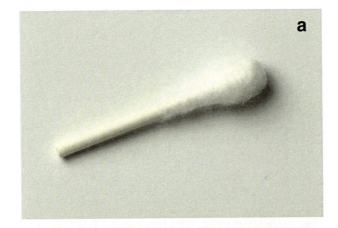

paint (no waste), plus makes your project "green". Reduce, reuse, recycle!

The paint brushes for this technique are just ingenious. Take Q-tips and cut them in half (photo a) to make 2 dip sticks. Solid paper Q-tip sticks are best. Cheaper swaps use hollow plastic tubes, which don't work as well.

Stencils are provided in appendix A. These are especially useful for younger children or for children who may need a starting point. Photocopy the outlines onto card stock and cut them out. Provide enough card-stock outlines for the group you are teaching; each child will need a few moments with the outline.

Procedure

1. Read examples of dot paint stories (see reference page) to the class to give them the idea. The students may or may not want to tell a story with their painting. I have seen some terrific stories painted...

2. If the student decides to use a card-stock outline, trace around the animal lightly with a pencil. This is easier to erase if there is a mistake. Remind them their own hands make a cool outline, too.

Once all students are pleased with the pencil outline, have them use a black Sharpie pen to follow the pencil line.

3. Now plan out the background of the painting in pencil, encouraging your students to use circles, wavy lines, or fields of color. Traditional aboriginal symbols are provided in appendix A.

4. Starting with the Sharpie pens (photo b), add stripes or color areas inside and outside the animal. This is done now, in case the students want to "dot" on the colored areas later.

5. Practice dot-making on a scrap paper first. Show the class how to grasp the

cotton end of the dipstick. Dip the cardboard stick into the paint. Point out it does not need to go in deeply at all - this will keep their brushes (and therefore their paintings) from getting "gunky". Photo c shows too little paint, this dot will be anemic. Photo d shows a good amount, photo e shows too much paint on the dip stick.

The dots are made cleanly and purposefully. The sticks come straight <u>down</u> and pause on the paper before being pulled straight <u>up</u> off the paper (photo f). The resulting dot should be round and even and cover completely (photo g, left). Too timid a dotting will leave an undersized or anemic dot (photo g, right). "Globbing" paint onto the dipstick will give over-sized or oddly-shaped blobs. A balance can be found between these two. Practice making one dot after the other. Be sure there is no "connection" between dots (photo h), caused by trailing the dipstick and not cleanly lifting the stick between dots.

6 Once the dotting technique has been practiced, let them loose on their "real" paintings. Start with the white dots and go through the palette one color at a time. With young kids, remind them **not** to lay their hands in wet dots while painting. These will take longer to dry than other styles of painting they may have done.

7 I have found most students need around 3 hours to finish a 12 x 12 inch painting. It works nicely to break it up into 3 separate hours (or separate days for younger children), allowing drying time in between. Older children have longer attention spans, but even adults go a little dizzy doing a whole painting in one sitting. Judge your group.

8 Allow the paintings to dry completely. Some dots may be standing up and need longer to dry than it looks at first glance!

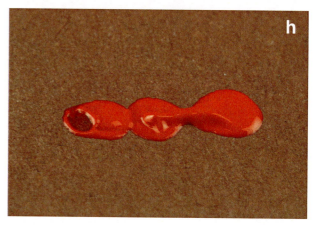

Afterthoughts

This technique just cries for fundraiser auction attention. Imagine an elementary classroom needing a project for an auction. Some Clever Art Docent goes to the thrift store and buys a used but stable wooden bookshelf unit and gives it a quick paint job in a nice new color. Then the kids are given card-stock outlines of... oh, I don't know... different sea animals, for example. The kids dot these animals all over the outside of the shelves and connect them up with dotted "wave" lines of water current in blue dots. (Here in the Pacific Northwest, this would be a Salmon Life Cycle bookshelf and probably would tie to the lesson plan in the classroom.) Each student could sign their sea animal and the newly attractive bookshelf could be auctioned at the fundraiser to the highest-bidding parent – or the highest-bidding art lover!

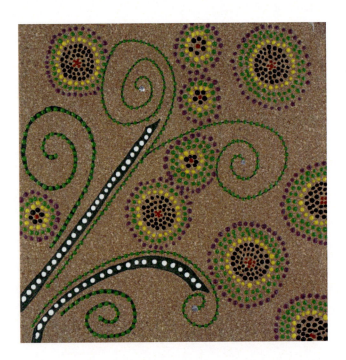

Creative Crafts of the World Aboriginal Dot Painting

Viking Knitting

This is a jewelry making technique using thin wire and simple looping around a dowel to create a complex-looking coil. This coil is then drawn through increasingly smaller holes in a wooden draw-plate to even out and lengthen the coil into a elegant necklace that no one would assume is easy to make.

History

Nearly 1300 years ago, the Vikings looped wire into a rope and then stretched the ropes to make jewelry for their powerful leaders. Numerous sources mention that examples of these chains have been found at various archeological sites in Scandinavia, dating back to the 8th century.

This looped wire chain is also called trichinopoly, but is more commonly called Viking Knitting. It is similar to knitting, in that it appears to be loops pulled through loops. However, the construction technique also has a lot in common with Nålebinding (Danish: literally "binding with a needle") in that the loops are made by manipulating the **end**, not the **middle**, of the strand.

This ancient craft provides you, as a teacher, with a great "teachable moment" by allowing you to slip in lots of history and geography lessons while your students are quietly looping.

Terminology

<u>Draw-plate</u>: Block of wood through which a number of ever-smaller holes are drilled (Starting at ⅜ inch and going down from there)

<u>Stitch-heads</u>: The upright loops of wire that will form columns on your dowel

<u>Neck</u>: The cross of the wire under the stitch-head (see graphic)

Materials

- Gauge 26 crafting wire, approximately 8 yards per student (the "good" wire)
- Gauge 26 black wire, approximately half a yard per student, to make the starting daisy. (This will be thrown away in the end.)
- ⅜ inch dowels cut to 12 inch lengths, one per student
- Plastic cards, such as old gift cards or credit cards
- Scotch tape
- Wire snips
- Eye protection, depending on the age of the students
- Wooden draw-plate, one per class is enough
- Small pliers for the pull
- Gauge 24 wire (for the findings)
- Size 7 knitting needle
- E6000 glue

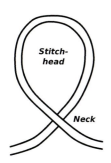

Creative Crafts of the World — Viking Knitting

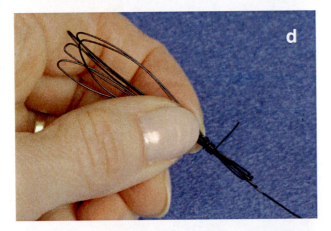

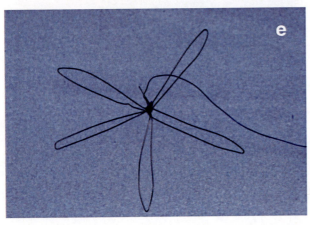

Class Preparation

This craft requires some dexterity and is best suited for middle-schoolers and up.

If your students are perfectionists, it may be useful to draw five parallel lines down the length of the dowel in permanent marker for the students to "aim" at (photo a).

Unwinding the wire from the package can be a bit challenging for excited students, and you might end up with an awful wire knot. This is the only problem I have ever had while teaching this class. You may want to have the wires already cut nice and straight and available for them.

I teach large numbers of kids, so I built myself a wire dispensing rack (photo b). Taking wire from this rack, the kids have less trouble with knots, provided they pull the wire from the **side** and not the top of the spindle.

Tell your class before they begin that we want to avoid kinks getting pulled tight in the wire. This will form a weak spot in the wire.

Procedure

1. Wrap the black (daisy) wire around the plastic card until there are five loops across the bottom (photo c). Slide the wire off the card and bind the bundle together with one end of the black wire about ¼ of the length from the end (photo d).

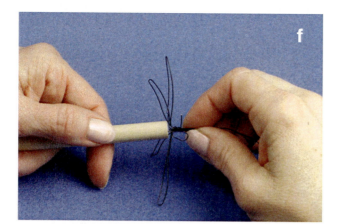

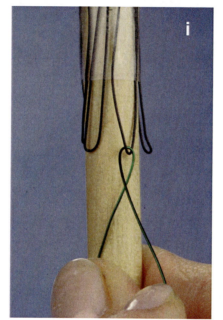
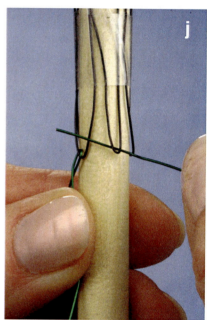

Open these "petals" up to make the starting daisy (photo e).

2. Lay the daisy face-down on the top of the dowel (photo f), and bend the petals down around the sides. Scotch tape them in place (with the ends sticking out) so the daisy won't fall off the dowel (photo g).

3. Introduce the "good wire" now. Cut a piece at a convenient length for the student. I use a length from the nose to the out-stretched finger tips. A short length will gather fewer kinks; a longer length will need to be spliced less often, so use whatever happy medium works for each student. Insert this wire from the left to the right through a petal of the daisy. Insert it about

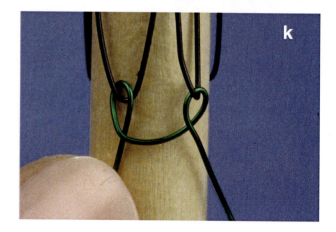

one inch (photo h) and bend it 'down' on the dowel. Take the remaining wire (the long side) and swing it to the right in front of the other wire, forming a stitch-head on the petal (photo i).

19

Creative Crafts of the World Viking Knitting

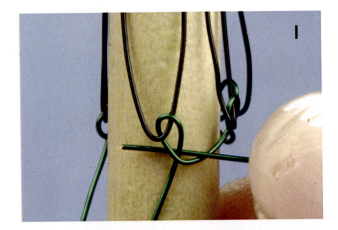

l

m

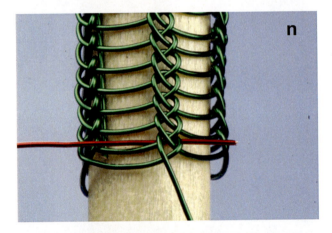

n

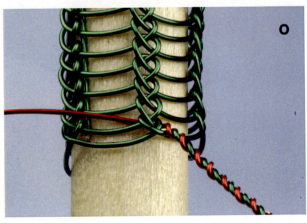

o

4 Now using the long end of the wire and holding the short end in place with your thumb, insert the good wire into the next petal to the right (photo j) from the right towards the left. Pull the length through and swing the wire to the right and over the wire you just laid to form a second stitch-head (photo k). Continue in this manner, entering a new petal for each stitch-head until all petals have been "lashed together" and you have five large stitch-heads around the bottom of the daisy.

5 Starting here, the student should continue inserting the long end of the wire from right to left in the direction of travel; but now instead of going into a petal, they should pass the wire behind the crossed wires that form a "neck" just under the stitch-head (photo l). Pull it through and swing it in front to the right as before. Tight work looks nice and even, but be sure they don't get it too tight to slide off the dowel when finished! If the tail is in your way it's okay to push it to the side – underneath of the growing coil (photo m).

6 Encourage the students to make evenly spaced, mostly straight columns of stitch-heads down the sides of the dowel. I can assure you, though, many wonky-looking works turn out looking great after being pulled through the draw-plate. This technique is very forgiving.

Splicing in a new wire

7 When the student's wire is running short (1 - 1½ inches) it's time to splice. Cut another workable length, and introduce it left to right (**Notice how all the stitches are taken from right to left except the introduction of a new piece; this one goes left to right!**) behind *not* the current stitch-head, but rather the stitch-head above. This is to ensure the new wire is secured to a "whole" stitch-head (photo n shows the new wire in red for visibility). Insert it about an inch and bend it down close to the ending

wire. Starting as close to the dowel as you possibly can, twist the wires tightly together (photo o) and lay them close to the dowel.

Photo p shows a good solid twist on the left and two examples of weak twists on the right. Watch your students carefully. A weak twist might not survive the draw-plate.

8. If you are confident the student has twisted cleanly and tightly enough, snip it off at about ½ an inch (photo q). Continue swinging and stitching as before (photo r). Pay special attention to the work until the tail of twisted ends is totally covered by stitching (photo s – shown in red only for visibility) which should happen within about five rows. This is important, because if the tail does <u>not</u> lay hard against the dowel, it's very tempting for young students to stitch <u>underneath</u> the tail. If the coil is pulled through the draw-plate in this way, the tail will stick out like a thorn (photo t). This *could* be a design element if you planned for it; students that are bored with "just the coil" as a necklace could make many of these thorns (and make them *long*). Then, after pulling through the draw-plate, add beads and such. Let their imaginations run wild!

9. One more note on the splicing; my finished dowel has a splice about once every inch. The tail of twisted ends can really be in the way for next few rows after a splice. It's OK to push the tail off to the side of the stitch column (photo s) to make it

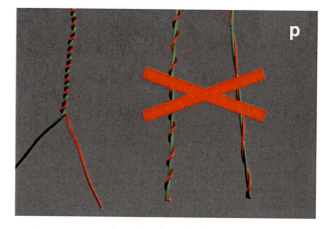

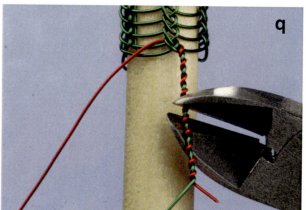

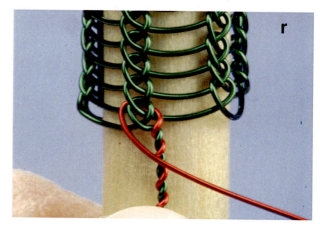

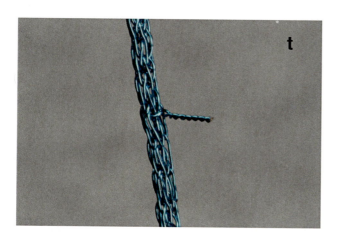

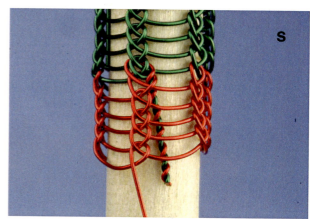

Creative Crafts of the World   Viking Knitting

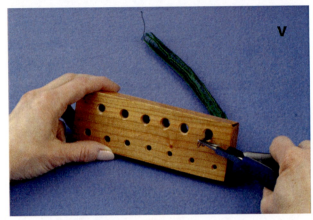

easier to get behind the neck on the next round. These tails are very hard to see (or even find!) in the coil once it has been pulled, so not to worry if there are many.

10 My students take two or three one-hour sessions to fill a dowel. Of course, if your class has the technique down, you can send the project home with lots of wire and have them bring it back (full) to your next class. Once the dowel is nearly full, start pushing it off the dowel (photo u) by starting at the bottom. The coil is vulnerable to being squashed once it is off the dowel; take it right away to the draw-plate.

11 Your draw-plate's largest hole should be the same size as the dowel you are working on. Starting with the largest hole (photo v), pull the coil through smoothly. The work will be more even. The kids love this part! Hole by hole, continue to pull the coil narrower (photo w) and longer. At some point, a pair of pliers are most helpful. Each student can decide which hole he or she wants to stop at; you don't have to go to the last hole. Once the coil is pulled, clip off the black daisy wire and discard (photo x).

12 To made the findings (hook and eye that will close the necklace), cut three pieces of gauge 26 wire at these lengths: 8 inches, 5 inches and 4 inches. Find whatever size knitting needle fits snuggly through the last hole the coil was pulled. Carefully wrap the long gauge 26 wire around the knitting needle and snip it in half to make the outer coiling for the two sides of the necklace (photo y). The other pieces are bent as shown in photo z and photo aa to make a hook and an eye, respectively.

13 If decorative beads are going on the necklace, this is the time to add them (photo bb). I have yet to see a bead

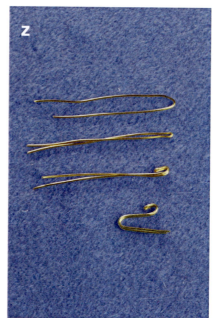
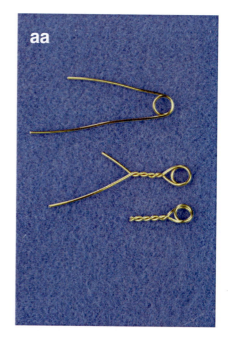
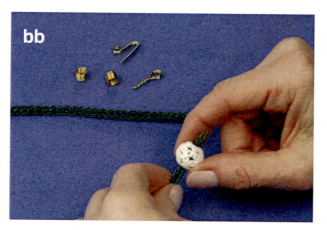

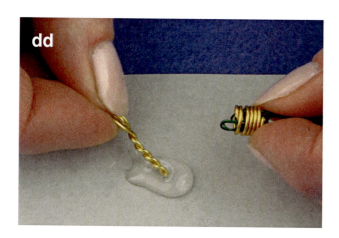

that would slide over the findings we are about to put on.

14 Do a test fitting to see if the findings fit on and into the necklace (photo cc). Please note that the hook and the eye are inserted **into** the knitted coil and the spring is **outside** the knitted coil. Disassemble again and roll the end of the hook and the eye in E6000 glue and re-assemble (photos dd and ee). Pick up enough glue with the hook and the eye to also glue the spring on the outside of the coil in place. Allow to dry undisturbed for 24 hours.

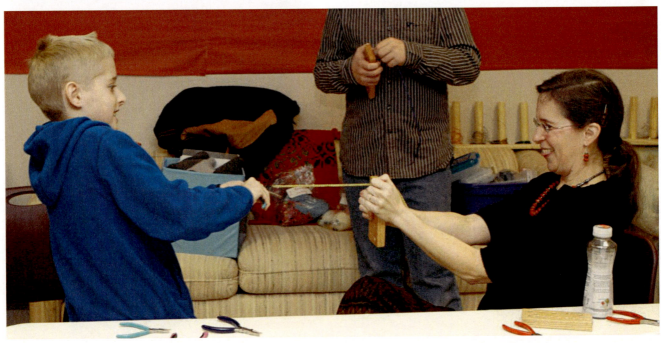

E6000 is serious stuff. With younger kids, I do this part, with older kids I emphasize how careful they must be to not get any on themselves and that they work with it only in good ventilation.

Afterthoughts

The necklaces make ideal Mother's Day gifts. Of course, bracelets can be made using the same technique. The resulting knitted coil is flexible enough that three coils could be braided together for an extraordinary necklace, too!

Stringed beads can be inserted into the coil if it is not pulled too narrow.

Huichol Beading

Here is a twist — a chance to use beads without textiles or thread. The glass beads are not used as jewelry or cloth embellishment, but rather to form a mosaic pattern decorating either the inside of a bowl or the outside of a wood form. My students do eggs at Easter in my class.

History

The Huichol are Native Americans living in the isolated Sierra mountains of Jalisco and Nayaril in Mexico. They decorate gourds as ceremonial drinking vessels for their gods. In their belief, the gods drink prayers from these vessels like we drink water. These bowls are called *jicara* (meaning gourd) in Spanish, or *kakure* in Huichol. In their artwork, the Huichol express their deepest religious feelings and beliefs. Their beading (as well as their yarn paintings) are a physical manifestation of their religious devotion.

Symbols that often appear in their work include maize (corn), the peyote flower, and deer.

Before they had access to glass seed beads, they used bone, clay, pyrite, shell, stone and seeds colored with insect dyes or vegetable dyes.

The bowls are decorated today by the Huichol with colorful glass beads pressed into bee's wax. They also do flat pictures with yarn pressed into bee's wax. These days the Huichol's art has become popular in many countries, and they have expanded beyond just gourd bowls to many shapes covered in delightful colors.

Materials

- Paper and colored markers for planning
- Coconut half-shells or half-gourds for decorated bowls or wooden egg shapes for Easter eggs
- Size 6 glass beads in many colors (bright colors are most traditional)
- Small bowls (to divide up the beads for multiple students if needed)
- Tacky glue
- Toothpicks, tweezers
- Newspapers or table drapes
- Moist paper towels to clean off the surface of the finished product

Creative Crafts of the World   Huichol Beading

Class Preparation

Seed beads vary widely in their quality. This project can be done with 'cheap' size 6 beads, but it will look better if done in seed beads from a shop specializing in beads rather than from a generic craft store. High quality beads will all be of the same height. Differences in the heights of the beads will show up in this project.

The Huichol use size 10 seed beads, and although this is lovely, my students have neither the patience nor the skill to work with such small beads. Depending on your situation, you may want to try the more delicate bead.

Procedure

1. This is a great, straight-forward craft for groups of kids. Show the students many examples of Huichol work for their inspiration (found on the internet, see resource page).

2. Protect the table surface with newspapers.

3. Have the students sketch the design they want to create on paper. This will evolve as the beads go on, but it's good to have a starting plan. Geometric patterns, especially triangles and hexagons work well, free-form shapes and pictures are more difficult in this technique.

4. If the project is a bowl, start the design in the very center (photo a). Put a medium layer of glue in a **small** area. Use a toothpick to place the beads and move them up close to their neighbors (photos b,d). Just the right amount of glue will have a little "grouting" of glue come up between the beads.

5. Sometimes if the space is too small, it is necessary to glue a bead on its edge.

Do not glue an area larger than the area you can cover with beads in one session (photo c). If the unused glue dries, it will prevent you from laying new beads close and flat the next time.

6. If the project is an egg instead of a bowl, start from the top point. Follow the advice above, but also watch for the egg's biggest challenge: when the glue layer is too thick, groups of beads will slide quietly downwards. Catch this before the glue dries.

7. During the session, frequently press the beads into the bowl (or onto the egg) to ensure a smooth, even finished product.

8. At the end of each session, clean the unfinished edges of the bead work with a toothpick to ensure that the next time you can start glueing onto bare surface. Gently wipe any excess glue off the piece with a wet paper towel.

My middle schoolers need about 3 to 4 one-hour sessions to plan and finish a 2.5 inch tall egg. The bowls take a little bit longer.

Afterthoughts

Eggs decorated in the Huichol technique, while not strictly traditional, are a lovely decoration or gift at Easter. The bowls are also lovely and useful, being a charming holder for earrings, bus fare, your mail box key, whatever you want!

d

Natural Dyes

Chemical dyes claim to offer all colors of the rainbow but can often end up looking artificial and sometimes garish. Contrast this with natural dyes that result naturally in warm, wholesome colors using a simple process. Kids love to watch this magic happen and are delighted to see they can get color from everyday materials.

History

Most kids these days do not realize that before 1856, all cloth color came from natural dyes. If you couldn't find it in nature, you didn't have that color.

And it started early: Egyptian mummies have been found in cloth dyed in madder root (red). The earliest *written* record of dyed cloth is from China in 2600 B.C. Indigo (blue) was used by the early inhabitants in England. When the Romans entered, they encountered the Picts (an ancient people) who used indigo for tattoos. This is where the word "Briton" originated. It means "painted men" in Latin. By the 10th century there was a wool dyers' guild (professional association) in Germany.

Dyeing was a skill every family needed before the Industrial Revolution made mass-produced cloth available.

In 1856, William Henry Perkin discovered the first chemical dye "mauve" (while searching for a cure for malaria!)

New Vocabulary

Dyestuff: A material from which color is extracted to place on fiber

Mordant: A chemical that helps a fiber accept dye

Exhausted dye bath: When all the color has been removed from the liquid by the wool

Hank: Yarn tied in a circle to prevent tangling

Skein: Yarn hank with twist put in it to compact it (see opposite page)

Resist dyeing: A substance (e.g. wax, clamps, or binding) applied to the surface of yarn to protect it during the dyeing process

Ikat dyeing: Threads bound on light colored yarn to offer a resist during the dyeing process

Materials

- 5 small hanks per student of bulky weight white 100% wool yarn (5 yards) OR worsted weight white 100% wool yarn (10 yards)
- Mordanting pot; enamel or stainless steel
- Spoon with long handle
- Alum
- Cream of tartar
- Measuring spoons
- 4 old crock-pots labeled "Dye Pot" (e.g. from thrift store)
- Dish soap
- Yellow onion skins (yellow exterior skins) - about four handfuls
- Mesh bag for onion skins, like the kind grapes are sold in
- Turmeric spice - about 2 Tablespoons
- Frozen or fresh blackberries - about two cups
- Dry black walnut hulls (about one cup) OR ten black tea bags
- Slotted spoons with long handles
- Old panty hose - 4 legs worth
- Permanent marker
- Plastic tags cut from milk jugs with holes punched used as labels
- Old salad spinner (optional) labeled "Dye"
- Plastic plates or cut bottoms of milk jugs for spoon-rests
- Plastic tubs for rinsing or access to a (non-porous) sink
- Plastic bags for sending home dyed skeins - they will be wet

Safety first

Dyeing is chemistry, and even though natural dyes are (mostly) much safer than chemical dyes, caution is the watchword when dyeing with kids. Use no heavy metal mordants (chrome, tin, etc.) The only mordant I use with kids is Alum, and since this is food-grade stuff, it is safe enough. All tools, pots, spoons used in dyeing should thereafter not be used for food preparation. I paint "DYE POT" on everything I bring to this class. The kids (depending on their ages) should be informed ahead of time that chemistry deserves respect and also that the pots will be hot. See to it that the dye pots are placed on stable tables. Personally, I place them right on the floor. Although there probably won't be a problem with splattering, play clothes on the kids are never a bad idea.

How It Works

Mordants are chemicals that help the dye molecule "bite on" to the wool (from the latin **mordere** to bite). Most dyes are more resistant to fading from light exposure or washing with a mordant pre-treatment on the yarn. However some dyestuffs contain natural mordants right in them – one-stop shopping! For example, rhubarb leaves, as a dyestuff, not only provide a light yellow color, but also have a strong mordant: oxalic acid. Thus, rhubarb leaves can be used as a mordant for a dyestuff with a stronger color, that then combines with the weak yellow. Oxalic acid is the reason your mom told you never to feed rhubarb leaves to your bunnies and by the way, it is very toxic. I do **not** use rhubarb mordant with children. Another (less toxic) natural mordant is tannin found in black walnut hulls. This gem of a dyestuff delights each of my classes with its deep chestnut brown color.

I have given instructions here for 4 colors plus white, but if your group enjoys dyeing, the possibilities are almost endless. See references for good books on the subject, or do what I did, and hike your local woods or backyard for "interesting" plant stuffs. You'll be surprised to find that pretty nearly everything gives some color. It may not be what you expect, either. Have your kids hypothesize (science lesson!) what color beets will give. (Spoiler Alert: It's not red!)

The dye procedure in this chapter is for 100% wool. Plant fibers (e.g. cotton, linen) require a very different dye process.

Class preparation

Winding the Hanks

a The yarn should be wound into a circle; over the backs of two chairs works well, around a large picture book is an alternative, and using a swift as shown in photo a is the best option if you have one.

b Yarn to be dyed must use a special tie-up to avoid "resist" dyeing. Resist dyeing happens when a portion of the dye hank is bound too tightly and the dye cannot easily penetrate under the tie. This actually leaves a white "stripe" in the yarn which is usually a mistake. (This "mistake" can be beautiful in the hands of a master dyer! Look up Ikat dyeing on the web, especially from Guatemala where it is called Jaspe, or Indonesia where the word Ikat originated.) To avoid the white stripe problem, the hanks are "bound" loosely using a dyer's knot as shown.

Tie the hank loosely in various points with the dyer's knot (photo b). Dyers use the word 'knot' differently than most people. A dyer's knot is yarn woven loosely through the hank and secured with an actual knot (square knot or overhand knot).

The two ends of the yarn can be secured with a very loose loop knotted in place.

Each student will get 5 hanks; One that has been mordanted with alum, three to dye un-mordanted, and one to leave white.

Mordanting (one hank per student)

The mordanting process can be shown to the kids or performed ahead of time by you. It's not real flashy, so I mordant ahead of time for my classes. My suggestion is you make up a lot of mordanted hanks while you are at it, since they can be dried, labeled, and stored and still remain mordanted indefinitely.

This mordanting procedure is for 100% wool yarn (or other animal fibers). Plant fibers like cotton are handled very differently; see references.

1. Weigh your hanks, write down how heavy they are for the next step. Soak them in water for 1-2 hours.

2. Make up a mordant bath in a large stainless steel pot. For each 4 oz of yarn, you will need 1¾ tsp. alum, 1½ tsp. cream of tartar (photo c) and 4 gallons of water. First dissolve each chemical in about ½ cup of boiling water; then add these solutions to the 4 gallons of cold water and stir with a long handled spoon.

3. Squeeze excess water out of the soaked hanks and add them to the cool mordant pot. Heat <u>slowly</u> to simmering (photo d). Do not boil. The reason we are so careful with rapid temperature change is to avoid the wool *felting*. We want that to happen in the felting chapter, but not here in the dyeing chapter!

4. Simmer for an hour, occasionally moving the hanks around gently to ensure the solution gets to all parts of the yarn. Do not let the yarn float to the surface for the same reason.

5. Turn off the heat and allow the pot and hanks to cool overnight, or at least 2 hours.
6. Remove the hanks and rinse thoroughly, and allow to dry.
7. Notice that these hanks look **exactly the same** as the un-mordanted hanks. Label them now as mordanted.
8. These mordanted hanks will all go into the turmeric dye pot (Pot 2)

Procedure

Setting Up the Dye Pots on Dye Day

Waterproof table drapes are very useful, or at the very least newspapers under all of this.

1 Fill 4 thrift store crock pots ¾ full with water and set on high 1-2 hours before the kids want to start dyeing. This class will need some time to prep and have the pots ready and bubbling for the kids when they arrive. I find it best to schedule this class in the middle or end of the school day; that way I'm able to get the pots up & going all morning.

2 To these dye pots add (for an estimated 10 students):

POT 1: 4 handfuls of dried onion skins in a mesh bag (photo e, the mesh bag is for easy removal).

POT 2: 2 Tbsp. turmeric spice (photo f) tied in the toe of a pantyhose foot (this smells nice while cooking!)

POT 3: 2 cups fresh or frozen blackberries (photo g) tied in a pantyhose leg.

POT 4: about 1 cup dried black walnut hulls tied off in a pantyhose foot (photo h) OR 10 black tea bags (Black walnuts give the nicer color. If you can get hulls, it's worth the effort. See references.)

3 Allow the pots to simmer about one hour.

4 Prepare a basin of *very* warm water with a touch of liquid soap to pre-soak the hanks, once the students have them labeled.

Here come the students!

5 Each student is given 5 hanks. Of these, one is mordanted and will go into POT 2 (turmeric). One of the un-mordanted hanks will *not* be dyed and remain white for comparison.

Each student should prepare 5 labels with permanent Sharpie pens as follows:

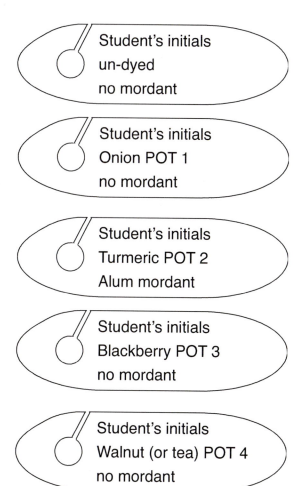

e

f

g

h

35

The onion skins will try to float

Black walnuts are anxious to give up color

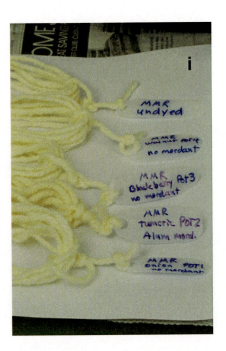

(Cut open a slot in the punched hole, to attach it to yarn skein)

6. Once hanks are labeled (photo i), call the students up with their "onion" hanks and have them wet them in the basin of very warm water and a drop of soap (photo j). Soap will break the surface tension and allow better wetting – and thereby better dye penetration – in the dye pot. It's all about not getting white spots. Squeeze out.

7. Ease the wet hanks into the onion pot – be sure none float above the surface! If your kids are old enough, one student could babysit the pot, gently moving the hanks around in the dye for even coverage (no need to stir – we aren't mixing here). If the pot is crowded, remove the dyestuff bag – this will be hot! – and discard. But if everything can move freely with the bag *in* the pot, it's best to dye together with the dyestuff. You will extract every last bit of color.

8. Repeat for "turmeric" hanks, blackberry hanks and walnut (or tea) hanks.

9. Simmer for about an hour, moving the hanks fairly occasionally.

See the following two pages for the process of the dyeing: in the top photos a piece of white plastic shows the dye pot color when it is ready for the wool. Next the hanks are shown in the pot, when removed after 5 minutes, and again after one hour. Left to right are Pot 1 (onion), Pot 2 (turmeric), Pot 3 (blackberry) and Pot 4 (black walnut).

Now is a good point to discuss any books you may have on natural dyeing with the class. Libraries have lots of these; also see reference list at the end of the book. Discuss with the class what colors could come from tree barks, blueberries, apple leaves in the spring, apple leaves in the fall (yes, there is a difference!), lily stamens, dark red flower petals, beets (try this one for sure – your kids may be fooled!). There is even an insect that gives natural dye: cochineal (red color). Have your older students do some

Creative Crafts of the World — Natural Dyes

research on this bug and its importance to Mexico in the 17th century for extra credit. For 200 years it was Mexico's third most important export to Europe, after gold and silver.

Maximize the time the hanks have in the dye pot. If you have only one hour with your class, that will have to do, but if you can leave the hanks in the dye pot to cool overnight you will get maximum color.

10 When you remove the hanks, be careful not to drip the dye liquid on any clothing. Rinse many times in water of a similar temperature until the rinse water runs clear. If you have one, an old salad spinner (labeled "DYE") can spin out a lot of water. Otherwise, blot the hanks in an old towel and send them home with the kids in plastic bags. Instruct them to hang the hanks to dry as soon as they get home; they will mildew in plastic if left wet. And the kids may want this yarn for our next project!

11 If the dye liquid went "clear" on you, the bath was exhausted. This is good; all the color potential latched on to the wool. If not, more yarn could be dyed with the amount of dyestuff you used. Would the teacher like to dye a few hanks? The pot can be re-heated at home. Do not try to transport the dye liquid hot (or even cold) inside the dye pot – mess potential. Once it's cool, it can be stored in an empty milk jug until it molds (black walnut can be used even **after** it molds!) and be reheated and reused.

Creative Crafts of the World

Natural Dyes

38

Creative Crafts of the World — Natural Dyes

From left to right: Un-dyed, the four pots: onion (1), turmeric (2), blackberry (3), black walnut (4). The left of the couplet being a 5 minute dye ('a'), the right being a 1 hour dye ('b').

Afterthoughts

I have chosen these four dye baths because they give me four high contrast colors; onions give orange, turmeric with alum mordant gives bright yellow, blackberries give light purple, and black walnut gives chestnut brown. If you have a neat color offered in one of your reference books from a flower or leaf you have access to, go for it! No natural dye "clashes" with another, no matter what you use.

An optional step you can use to get a larger variety of colors with just these four dye pots is to give a quick simmer to the dyed yarn in a cast iron pot or frying pan (again from a thrift store). The iron will "sadden" the colors. If you are planning to do this step, dye *two* hanks per student per dye pot in the procedure above, then once they are done, leave one skein "bright" and "sadden" the second.

There is no end to the fun and exploration available to the young natural dyer! Check out the resource books for even more after-treatments (and even some pre-treatments) used to further expand your range of color!

Creative Crafts of the World   Natural Dyes

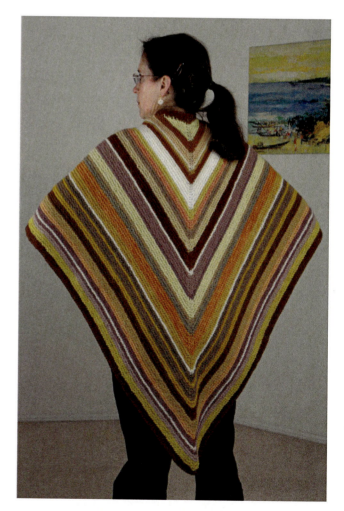

Weaving

The little bags we weave in this project are a fashion hit with 1001 uses! Cell phone case, coin purse, project bag, paperback book tote, Mother's Day gift…

Creative Crafts of the World — Weaving

History

Weaving goes *way* back. The development of string appeared in the upper Paleolithic period in central Europe. But we had to wait until 8000 -7000 B.C. for woven cloth to be created.

The direct precursor to what became the loom we use today was the horizontal ground loom. For this, stakes are driven into the ground and wooden beams are lashed to them. The warp is stretched horizontally between the beams staked a few inches above the ground. Many ancient people used the horizontal ground loom (and the Bedouins still use it enthusiastically today).

The addition of heddles to hold groups of warp threads, as well as the development of pedals to lift them, had the early loom looking significantly like the foot loom that hand weavers use today.

For this class, we revert back to the horizontal loom, even if it is a very small version of it that sits on the table, not the ground!

New Vocabulary

Warp: Threads held parallel and under tension on a loom

Weft: Threads that are woven through the warp threads at 90 degrees

Shed: The space created when some of the warp threads are raised, through which the weft thread is passed

Shuttle: Tool that carries the weft through the shed

End: One warp thread

Ends per inch: Measurement of spacing of warp-ends

Pick: One pass of the weft thread

Plain weave: Weave structure where the weft goes over-under, over-under through

Materials

Loom Construction:
- Foam Board ½" thick (or wood ¼" thick)
- Wood glue
- Duct tape
- Wide tooth combs 3 or 4 per loom
- Scissors
- Large paint stir sticks
- Access to saw for cutting paint-sticks / wood

Weaving:
- Warp yarn (Lamb's Pride or worsted). Bulky is best for youngsters, older students can handle the finer yarn.
- Duct tape
- Hair pick for beater
- Shuttle or long plastic needle
- Scissors
- Five skeins dyed in previous chapter (or commercial yarn in various colors).
- Large-eyed needle to hide ends
- Fringe twister (optional)

Creative Crafts of the World — Weaving

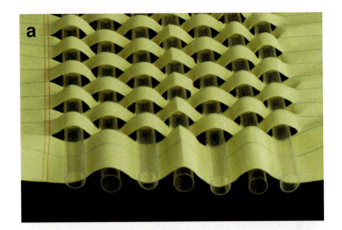

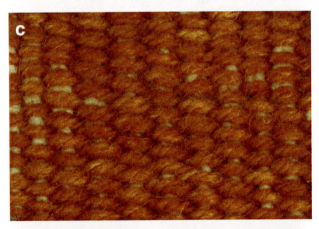

the warp, showing both warp and weft in a balanced ratio.

<u>Weft-faced weave</u>: Weave structure where the weft thread shows and the warp thread is covered.

<u>Beat</u>: To compact weft picks with a beater tool

<u>Selvage</u>: The two sides of a weaving (left and right sides on this loom) that will not unravel

Background

In the final weaving the weft threads will undulate over and under the warp threads, just as the paper 'weft' undulates over and under the straws simulating the warp in photo a. The look and feel (not to mention the width!) of the woven fabric will change quite dramatically, depending on how much space the weft thread is given for this.

When *straws* are warp, they will not undulate. When *yarn* is warp, the warp threads can undulate a bit, too. If the warp threads are placed close to each other and the weft is beaten such that the number of picks per inch equals the number of ends per inch, both warp and weft threads undulate equally and the result is balanced plain weave (photo b).

On the other hand, when the warp threads are father apart and the weft thread is less taut, the weft thread will have more opportunity to undulate and will cover up more (or even all) of the warp (photo c). The resulting fabric is called a weft-faced plain weave.

Class Preparation

Loom Construction

Depending on the age of your group, the looms can be made by the students themselves or by a helpful adult ahead of the class.

Cut very stiff foam board (½" thick) to approximately 10" X 24" (photo d). Wood can also be used if you don't mind the weight.

Cut paint stir-sticks to 10". These are glued and duct-taped to each end of the top side of the loom (photo e) to raise the warp threads up off the foam board for easier weaving.

Tape combs onto the *bottom* of the foam board hanging over approximately ¾" as in photo f. Tape these securely, pull tight, overlap onto the front and secure well (photo g).

These are sturdy multi-use looms (photo h), once constructed they can either be held and used next year with new students or the students can take them home to weave future projects.

These looms were developed by Barbara Matthiessen in her book *Small Loom &*

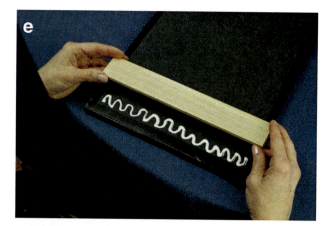

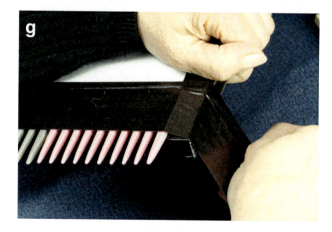

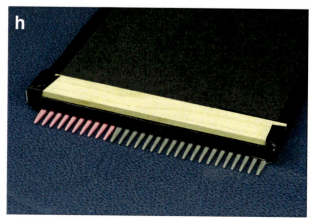

Creative Crafts of the World   Weaving

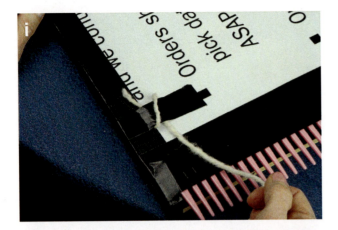

Freeform Weaving published by Creative Publishing international. If your kids enjoy the project in this chapter, they will like everything in her book, too!

Procedure

Warping the loom

1. Attach one end of the yarn to the loom with duct tape. It's important that this end not come loose. Wind it once around the duct tape to secure it before placing the tape (photo i).

2. Wind the yarn around the loom lengthwise spacing evenly by using the comb's teeth (photos j and k). You want approximately 4 ends per inch using the bulky or approximately 6 ends per inch using the worsted. More ends per inch will result in plain weave, fewer ends per inch will allow weft-faced cloth.

3. End the warp thread as you began it by taping it to the back of the loom. Now the loom is warped (photo l)

4. Insert a piece of the card stock (2" x 10") into the warp by alternately slipping it under one warp thread and over one warp thread (photo m). This will be the platform the weaving will be beat against.

Weaving

5. Thread your shuttle with a comfortable length of the yarn from one of your weft skeins (photo n). Weave the shuttle

above and below alternating warp threads (photo o). Make sure the warp threads going **under** the card go **over** the shuttle and vice versa, creating *opposite* sheds. Leave approximately 6" of the weft hanging hanging out of the warp as a tail (photo p). This tail is then inserted in the second pass.

The manner the weft thread lays in the shed before it is beaten in is very important. If the weft pick is simply pulled straight across the warp threads and pulled tight with no extra length for the weft, there will be a problem. The weft needs extra length so it can undulate between warps as we saw in photo a. If you are stingy with the weft, it will end up just *taking* the length it wants by pulling in the sides of the cloth (the selvages) and you end up with an hourglass shaped cloth. This shape is the hallmark sign of a inexperienced weaver and you will have to be diligent reminding the students to "leave the bubble" (photo q) to avoid this hourglass effect.

6 To make the bubble, pull the weft thread out the other side of the warp threads at about a 30 degree angle (photo p) and then pull the weft down to the card (photo q).

7 Once the weft shot has been bubbled and beaten down with the hair pick (photo r), the entire length of the tail is inserted by hand in the opposite shed (going over where the first pick went under and under where the first pick went over).

47

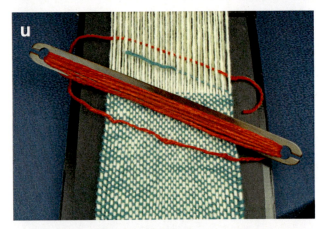

From the other side, the shuttle will also make the opposite shed. Obviously for approximately 6" there will be 2 weft threads in this shed. Not to worry; these will mesh down as the cloth is beaten.

8 Continue weaving with the shuttle alternating sheds each pick.

9 Here's a slick tip to cut your work in half! Insert a stick in the warps at the top of the loom in one of the sheds (photo s). Warp tension will hold it in place. Now when you come to the "freebie" shed just slide the stick down towards your weaving and stand it up. No more pick and dive, just pass the shuttle through the new channel! (photo t). After you make the bubble, lay the stick down again, then slide it up and out of your way for the pick-and-dive shed.

Note: There is a way to cut your work even further using a stick and string heddles (you get two freebie sheds). Although some students figure it out by themselves, I do not teach this because it tends to confuse more students than it helps. You could tell them it is possible and have them research the trick to report on it back to the group.

It's also fine if your goal is to teach them to weave cloth and not to make them little inventors. For that, the one pick-and-dive shed and one freebie-shed method is just fine.

10 When the length of weft runs out, or when you want to change colors, "bubble" the last bit of your of weft and leave a length hanging out of the shed on the top of the weaving. This tail will later be hidden with a needle. Introduce your new weft into the *same* shed and be sure the 2 threads overlap for a bit (approximately 2" or 3"). Once again there will be 2 threads in the same shed for a time. Leave a tail of new weft hanging out on top of the weaving as well, to be hidden later (photo u) in either the next pick or with a needle

after weaving. Beat and continue weaving as before.

11 Weave until the new cloth is approximately 14" long, helping the kids remember all along to watch for the hourglass problem.

I have my students make a bag with their cloth, although thick wool cloth also makes a nice trivet. Use your own judgement.

12 Hide the warp-ends before you cut the cloth off the loom. Each warp-end will be threaded through a large tapestry needle and worked into the cloth somewhere *other than* it's own warp-end channel. The next channel over works well. Clip the end carefully, close to the cloth but not snipping any weft threads.

Hide all internal tails too. These may be quite short, so show the kids the trick of hiding the needle first in the cloth and then threading the short tail into the needle before pulling it through.

13 Once the cloth is finished, the sides can be whip stitched together and a braided handle added to complete the bag. Refer to the twining chapter instructions for finishing the bag.

Afterthoughts

Kids have a very different relationship with cloth once they have woven their first piece. They appreciate the work and look at a handwoven piece with new eyes.

I have my kids weave this project using the yarn they dyed in the previous chapter. Boy are they proud!

Baumschmuck

In Germany and Austria, a charming folk art is prepared for the Tannenbaum: decorations made of wood, seeds, spices, beads and ribbon in geometric arrangements. These handmade treasures are natural and organic, easy enough for the youngest children, and a great gift idea.

History

Evergreen trees have been used since ancient times to celebrate the winter solstice as a symbol of the anticipation of the green spring. Evergreens were brought into the celebration of Christ's birth in Germany in the late middle ages, where people used small candles on the trees for lights. The tradition most probably came to the U.S. shores with German immigrants to Pennsylvania and Ohio.

Today the tradition of using real flames on the tree is still practiced in Germany (most German houses are stone, not wood!) These ornaments were a natural result of adorning the tree with things found "at hand".

New Vocabulary

<u>Tannenbaum</u>: German for pine tree

<u>Baumschmuck</u>: German for "tree jewelry"

<u>Christbaum</u>: German for Christmas tree

Materials

- Wooden bases in various shapes - purchased in craft stores, "Bottle Tops" game pieces, etc. You can also cut 1"- 2" branches into slices on a band saw.
- Tacky glue or regular white wood glue
- Toothpicks to move seeds into place in the glue
- Seeds - sunflower
    pumpkin
    honeydew
    tapioca pearls
    popcorn
    indian corn
    beans, etc.
- Spices - cinnamon sticks
    whole cloves
    mustard seeds
    whole star anise
    whole peppercorns, etc.
- Small acorns
- Red glass beads(#6)
- Red or green cording
- Scissors
- Pinch clips (optional)
- Paper plates (to transport home)
- Table drapes

Creative Crafts of the World   Baumschmuck

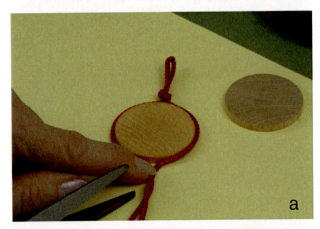
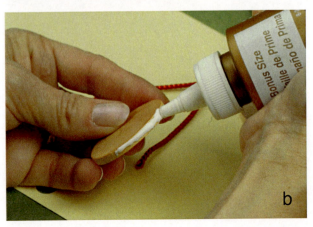

Class Preparation

A few comments on base shape; round always works and is easiest. Younger groups should use the round shape exclusively. It's also more traditional. There are other Christmas themed wooden shapes out there. It is very difficult to glue the cord around these. Students with great patience have managed the star successfully. Please note the middle picture on the previous page. For this star I used round cord and it worked out well, but it took some patience. Flat ribbon would be easier. Past experience proved other shapes to be too difficult.

Procedure

1. Take a piece of the cord long enough to go around the base plus 3 inches. In the middle, put a slip knot or overhand knot. (This will be where you hang your tree hook). Wrap it around the base and cut it leaving ½ inch extra on both sides (photo a).

2. I find attaching the cord *before* decorating works best for my students. Run a line of glue around the outside of your wooden base (photo b). Lay the cord into the glue line and pinch the ends together (photo c) where they meet. This can be held with a clip if you like (photo d). After just a bit, you will be able to cut the ends and lay them into the glue for a seamless join.

Take care not to stretch the cord if it happens to be elastic. If the cord stretches and is cut before it dries, you will end up with a gap (photo e).

3. Lay out seeds and spices in geometric patterns (photo f). Show your students some examples and watch as they each come up with cool ideas you hadn't thought of. Some of my students have written their names out in wild rice!

4. Allow to dry.

Creative Crafts of the World · Baumschmuck

5 The next day, decorate the other side if desired.

Afterthoughts

Grandparents and aunts, school teachers and bus drivers, love to get these as Christmas gifts!

These look fantastic on the tree together with strands of hand-strung cranberries and popcorn – one of my favorite memories from my childhood growing up in the American Mid-west.

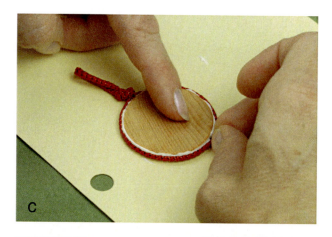
c

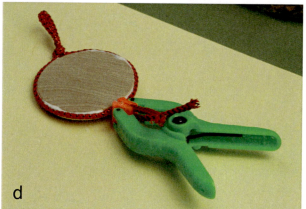
d

e

f

Creative Crafts of the World   Baumschmuck

Creative Crafts of the World   Baumschmuck

Paper Stars

Delightfully easy and deceptively complex! Just right for kids, adults, or anyone with a window that needs something pretty hanging in it!

History

These stars are popular in Europe, especially at the Christmas time when they are hung in windows. There they are made with a neat paper that looks and feels for all the world like waxed paper but that comes in a rainbow of bright colors. These days you can get anything off the web – you can order this paper from Germany (see resources) or you can use tissue-paper as a passable alternative.

The pattern inside the star comes from the different number of layers of translucent, colored paper. This comes from two things: the folding done to make up the component parts, as well as the overlap *between* the component parts.

New Vocabulary

<u>Papiersterne</u>: The German word for this craft "Paper Stars"

<u>Drachenpapier</u>: Colored wax paper from Germany

Terminology

<u>Sub-unit</u>: one square of paper, folded according to the drawings on the following pages

Materials

- Drachenpapier (see references) or tissue paper
- Fun foam sheets
- Scissors for each student
- Many extra rulers
- Sharp pencil for each student
- Paper folder tool (optional)
- Glue-sticks
- Scotch tape and thread for hanging

Class preparation

Although older students can handle measuring and cutting exact squares with pencils and rulers, I find with younger students – or with any age students where time is limited – using square foam templates is a great short cut.

Cut precise squares from fun foam, 3 inches on a side, one per student (photo a).

The paper used in Europe for this craft is a cool cross between waxed paper and tissue paper. It is basically colored heavy waxed paper. It can be purchased in the US (see references) over the Web, although a trip to Europe to get it is more fun! It is called 'Drachenpapier' (kite paper) in German. A passible alternative is tissue paper, but take great care not to treat the tissue-paper stars roughly.

These stars are shown in order of increasing difficulty. Judge the age of your group to decide how far they can go.

Procedure

Have the students choose a color and trace the foam template (photo b) for the number of sub-units needed for the star they are building. Rulers are a very handy way to keep the paper from rolling up on you (photo c).

Follow the folds in the diagrams to create a sub-unit. Repeat until all paper squares are folded into the correct sub-unit. After each fold, a small dab of glue stick under the fold will hold it in place. Construct the star from its sub-units as shown on each page.

Add thread with tape and hang in the window for best viewing.

Afterthoughts

This craft holds a lot of potential for fun lessons in math and geometry! Many, many stars are possible. Encourage your students to experiment and innovate.

Star 1 (Variation a)

Star 1 has two variations. The variation on this page has 8 sub-units.

Folding of a sub-unit
- Fold the square diagonally.
- Open it to a square again
- Fold corner A to lie on the diagonal and glue
- Repeat with corner B

Constructing the star
- Place the centers together. Rotate the lower left edge of the next sub-unit to lie on the diagonal fold of the sub-unit underneath as shown.
- Glue in place

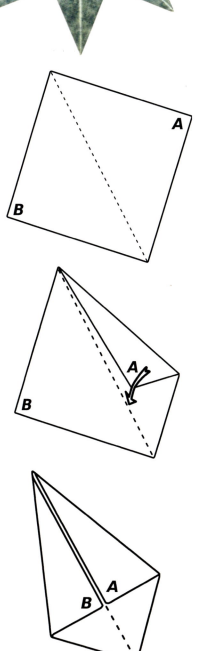

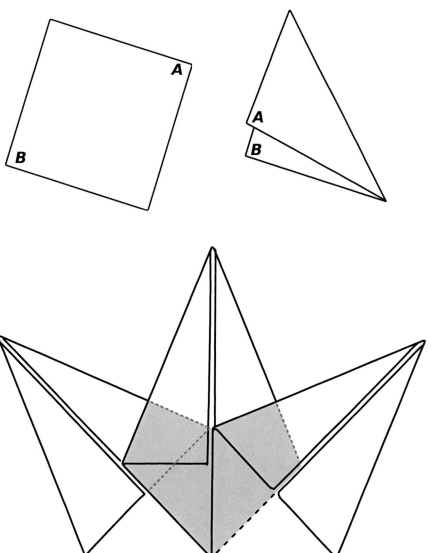

Star 1 (Variation b)

This is the second variation of Star 1. It uses 10 sub-units made identically to the sub-units of variation a, but then is constructed with more overlap.

Folding of a sub-unit
- Fold the square diagonally.
- Open it to a square again
- Fold corner A to lie on the diagonal and glue
- Repeat with corner B

Constructing the star
- Place the centers together. Rotate the sub-units as shown in the diagram. Notice that after three sub-units are placed, their bottom edges do **not** form a straight line as in variation a.
- Glue in place. Try to get the overlaps even around the star. If you work efficiently you can undo and adjust the arrangement before the glue dries.

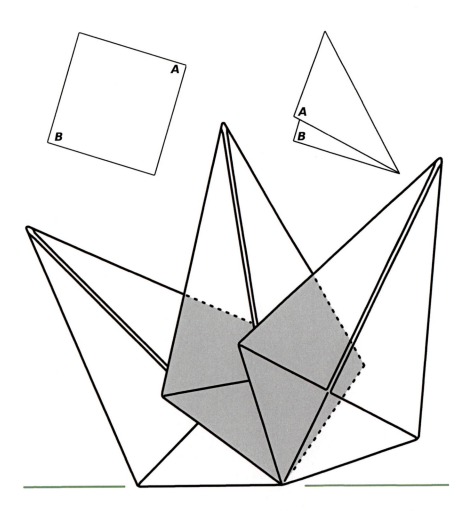
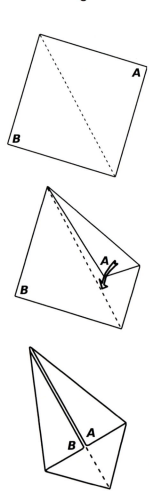

Star 2

This star uses 5 sub-units folded as seen below (purple star). Two completed stars can be superimposed to make a 10-pointed star (orange star).

Folding of a sub-unit
- Fold a sub-unit for Star 1
- Open it to a square again
- Fold corner B to the closest fold line
- Continue folding in the same direction to hide corner B inside the layers ("double fold trick") and glue in place.
- Repeat for corner A

Constructing the star
- Place the centers together. Rotate the sub-units as shown in the diagram. The angle of overlap will be very similar to the angle of the triple layer of each sub-unit.
- Glue in place. Try to get the overlaps even around the star. If you work efficiently you can undo and adjust the arrangement before the glue dries. In the end the star should lay flat.

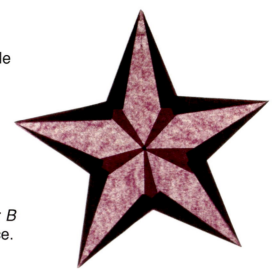
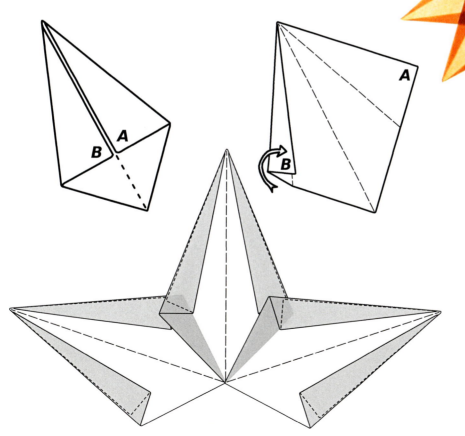
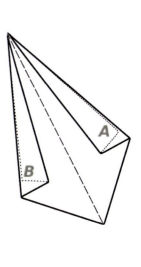

Creative Crafts of the World — Paper Stars

Star 3

This star uses 10 sub-units folded as seen below.

Folding of a sub-unit
- Fold a sub-unit for Star 1
- Fold the outside corners (C,D) to the diagonal fold and open up again. Please note that the crease line must start at the corner (E), the one with a single layer of paper
- The outside corners (C,D) are then folded to this new fold-line in preparation for the double-fold trick as in Star 2
- Fold again in the same direction (putting corners C,D inside the pocket) and glue

Constructing the star
- Place the centers E together. Rotate the sub-units as shown in the diagram. The overlap between the sub-units matches the width of the triple fold. Adjust before the glue dries.

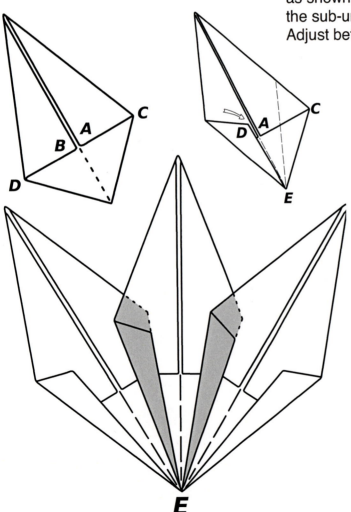
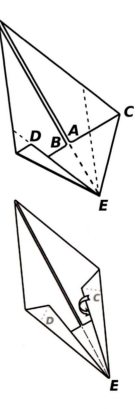

Block Printing

No other class I teach inspires more enthusiasm! The next week the kids all come to school proudly wearing T-shirts designed and printed by their own hands.

History

Long before Gutenberg invented movable type for the printed word (in 1450 A.D.), the Chinese were using carved wood blocks to print text and images on paper and fabric. The earliest surviving examples are from the Han Dynasty. This was more than 1200 years earlier!

In modern times, India and Pakistan have brought this technique to the level of a fine art.

Class Preparation

I do this craft over two separate days because I have the students for only 50 minutes at a time. You may be luckier and have a longer block of time. On day one we look through folk art books for inspiration. Then the students design and construct the printing blocks. While the glue for the printing blocks dries, we make rough sketches of how the designs will be put on the T-shirts. This planning stage is important for young ones. Then on the second day the paint comes out. Table drapes or lots of newspaper for this day are essential.

I always have the kids print with black fabric paint. I have tried other colors for block printing and have been sadly disappointed. Lighter colors often do not print solid in the kids' hands and the T-shirt color shows through unevenly. I've found the best way to guarantee success is to add color by having bright T-shirts and the black paint with simple designs that look clean and authentic.

Materials (Day 1)

- 1 or 2 brightly colored T-shirts per student (cotton or cotton/poly)
- Patterns from books or the web showing simple ethnic designs
- Various blocks of wood approximately 2" x 2" x ¾"
- Elmer's or Tacky Glue
- Fun foam sheets
- Scissors (for younger students)
- X-ACTO knives (for older students)

Materials (Day 2)

- Styrofoam meat trays (washed) or plastic lids for paint trays
- Foam brushes (approx. 1 per student)
- Soft fabric paint (Tulip brand)
- Skewers or popsicle sticks
- Aprons for kids or play clothes for stamping day
- Table drapes
- Newspapers
- Blocks made the day before

Creative Crafts of the World — Block Printing

This technique can be performed with carved potatoes, too. I use fun foam because the potatoes don't store well for next year's class!

The fun trick with block printing is that small pieces can build up to a larger whole. Note the short blocks (photo a) used to make the stripes and borders on this T-shirt (photo b). Inspiration for this T-shirt came from this African bedspread.

Procedure

1. Once the idea for a printing block is firm, students sketch it full sized onto a piece of fun foam with pencil or Sharpie. Encourage the kids to keep the pattern simple, and remind them that it will be in one color and the color will be black.

2. Cut the fun foam shapes and glue them onto the wood blocks (photos c & d). Allow to dry under a light-weight object for the best hold.

3. Younger students cut the fun foam with scissors. Older students can use X-Acto knives (photos e & f) to make more complex patterns.

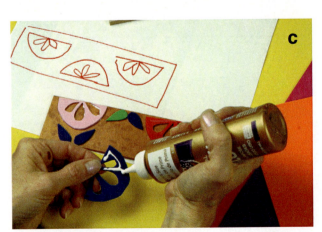

Creative Crafts of the World Block Printing

In this example, taking inspiration from the cover of the book, I am playing with positive and negative space. One block is the negative of the other.

Older students can have their printing blocks interact with each other geometrically. With some printing blocks, interesting patterns can be made by turning the block 90 degrees every time it is printed. See photo m at the end of the chapter.

Have the students plan the placement of their printing blocks first on scratch paper before they print on fabric.

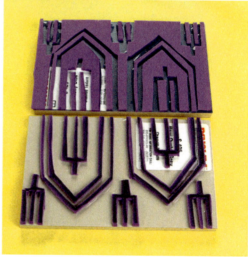

Professional printers in India use intermeshing printing blocks with different colors.

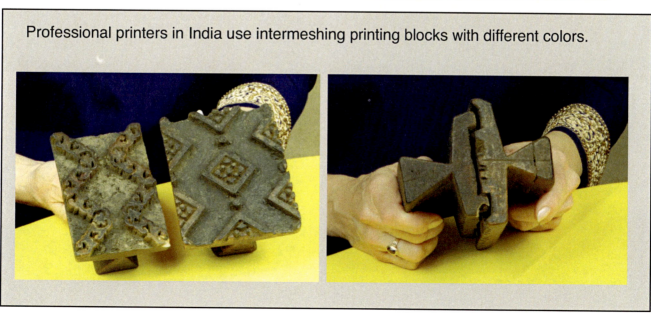

67

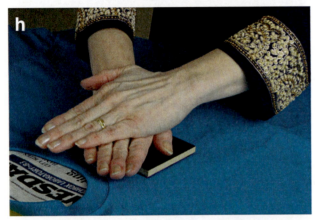

4. When the glue on the printing blocks is dry (in my class it is Day 2) it is time for the paint to come out! Table drapes and play clothes, please. Lay the T-shirts out flat on the tables or if need be, on the (covered) floors. It's important that the kids have enough space and are not bumping elbows. Each T-shirt should have flat newspapers inside as this will keep the front design from bleeding through to the back. Watch that the kids have the newspaper inside the shirts *very* flat. If there is a 'bunch', only the fabric over the bunch will get paint.

Squeeze 1 or 2 tablespoons of black fabric paint into a styrofoam meat tray or plastic lid.

5. Demonstrate good block-inking technique to the students. Very important: apply a thin, even layer of paint to all the print surfaces of the block using a 'pat pat' motion (photo g) and not a 'swipe swipe' motion. *Swiping* the paint on will fill in all the gaps with paint and then the paint will flow from these gaps onto the cloth during the printing. If paint does get in the gaps, clean it out as best you can with a skewer or popsicle stick.

An alternative inking method is squirting the paint out onto a sheet of glass, rolling it out thin with a tiny paint roller and using the glass like a stamp pad. However for economy and kid-friendliness, use the foam brush method.

6. Once all the inking surfaces are "loaded" (easy to tell, since they will be shiny and wet), demonstrate the correct printing technique:

1. Lay the printing block straight down onto the T-shirt.
2. Apply gentle, even pressure and count to 5 slowly. (photo h)
3. Lift the printing block straight up without shifting it sideways.

Sometimes you want to print only a part of a block. A useful trick for this is a strategically placed piece of newspaper (photos i and j) to mask the T-shirt.

7. If the pressure or the inking was uneven and the print is missing a part or if it is an anemic print (photo k), my advice is **not** to try to print it again in the same spot. You almost never get it spot-on and you will end up with a double image. This looks worse than the incomplete print. I have the kids fix bum prints later when the shirt is dry

with careful filling in using a Sharpie (T-shirt is lined again with newspapers, of course, photo l).

Print the entire plan on the front of the shirt. Backs can be done too, of course, but I advise you wait and do that after the front is all dry. Allow to dry 2 to 3 hours depending on thickness of paint.

Trays and brushes can be discarded if the situation requires quick and easy clean up, however both can be rinsed, dried and used again. The paint is water-soluble only while still wet. Reduce, reuse, recycle!!

Creative Crafts of the World — Block Printing

Afterthoughts

Commercial foam blocks are also available at craft stores (Michaels, Jo-Ann stores) and what's more, it is fun to find things to use as printing blocks. Anything with a cool texture in relief can be used as long as it can get wet.

Since this is a thriving craft even today in India, the internet is a fantastic resource for you, the teacher. YouTube offers many videos of wooden blocks being carved and used (see references).

Suggest to your class that the same techniques (even the same blocks!) can be used on paper to make hand-printed cards, wrapping paper, wall paper, etc! For this, other colors besides black work as well.

Advanced Block Printing

Printing with black paint gives consistently good results. However, other colors also can prove interesting for a smaller class or older students. Below you see how white color on a black background results in a see-through effect. Below that, gold printed *on top of* black gives a gilded feel.

Pysanky

Possibly nothing says "folk art" with such grace and delicate beauty as the incredible Ukrainian Easter egg!

Creative Crafts of the World — Pysanky

History

No actual examples of prehistoric Pysanky exist – eggshells are fragile! But this folk art does go back to ancient pagan times where the egg was a symbol of 'life after death'. It was decorated with many symbols of sun worship in anticipation of Spring after a cold winter. Ceramic eggs decorated like Pysanky have been found in prehistoric graves and are thought to represent the actual eggs.

With the acceptance of Christianity in Ukraine in 988 A.D. the egg took on the symbolism of Christ's resurrection and was decorated accordingly. The oldest real egg shell Pysanka ever found was a complete (although crushed) eggshell in the Baturyn excavation (razed in 1708).

In the 20th century Pysanky was banished in Ukraine by the Soviet Regime as a religious practice and nearly was forgotten. Museum collections were sadly destroyed during wars and by the Soviets. After the fall of communism, the folk art was revived and has enjoyed great popularity at home and admiration elsewhere in the world.

Materials

For each student:
- Raw eggs
- Kistkas and blocks of black or yellow wax (see resources page)
- Metal caps to lay hot kistkas on
- Small candles, matches & hair tie-backs
- Ukrainian Easter egg dyes (see resource page) - 3 colors for younger kids, possibly more for older students.
- Empty yogurt cups for carrying eggs
- Optional: an egg lathe for the class to use, to make smooth straight lines around the egg

For the instructor :
- Wide mouth mason jars (one for each color)
- Lots of egg cartons - paper cartons absorb best
- Rubber gloves and apron
- Slotted spoons or wire-basket strainers
- Lots of paper towels and a few small paper plates
- Newspaper or table drapes
- Hair dryer or embossing tool or candle
- Wide dish of dry "waste" rice if using the embossing tool
- Bead reamer or electric Dremel tool (better)
- Egg blower pipe
- Empty syringe without needle (500 ml)
- Large bowl to catch egg "insides"
- Spray polyurethane finish
- Metal findings to hang eggs and E6000 glue

Creative Crafts of the World — Pysanky

The lovely eggs are given to family members as well as respected outsiders, and are displayed prominently in the public room of people's homes.

New Vocabulary

<u>Pysanky</u>: Decorated eggs made in the Ukraine at Easter

<u>Kistka</u>: Hand-held tool that holds molten wax

<u>Exhausted dye bath</u>: Dye bath without enough dyestuff to sufficiently color an egg

Class Preparation

- The dyes are made up according to their directions the day before and allowed to cool back to room temperature.

- Cover your tables with newspaper or table drapes. I prefer newspaper or paper towels for the cushion – as well as the practice drawing surface – they offer.

- Each student will need their own kistka and their own candle and black wax. If necessary two students can share a candle and the wax. I find three layers of paper towels give the students the right space, and the towels will help the eggs NOT roll off the table when students lay them down. Each student will need a metal cap (jar lid or the like) on which to lay their kistka when hot (photo a).

- The dye table should be manned by an adult if you're working with young students. Waterproof table drapes are a must. Each dye needs a wide, open-mouthed jar or bowl and a slotted spoon for retrieving eggs. A disposable paper plate for a spoon rest is good – these dyes are for keeps on furniture and carpet.

- Young students can handle raw eggs if it is explained to them that they must be careful. It is possible to blow the egg guts out first and do this process with eggshells, but I don't. The eggshells break **much** easier in the kids' hands than the full eggs. Then there is the pain of having to somehow submerge a hollow egg in the dye, as well as having the eggshell dribble dye everywhere once it comes out... Of course, if we decorate full eggs and *then* 'drill, blow and gut' there is always a chance of someone's treasure breaking, but personally I have lost very few eggs in the drill & gut step. Many more eggs have broken in excited transport from the waxing table to the dyeing table when the students forgot to carry them in yogurt cups.

- The hardest part of teaching this technique to kids is the backwards logic used in the dyeing; it *looks* like you are putting black lines onto a white egg, but by covering some areas of a white egg, you are actually *protecting* the areas you want to stay **white**. Later it will be dyed **yellow**, and so on. Have patience with them understanding this weird logic – it will probably catch you, too.

Procedure

Check the eggs carefully. Any found to have subtle cracks, even if they appear robust, should be used for breakfast instead.

1 Have the students plan out how they want to decorate the eggs. See appendix B for suggested traditional symbols for Pysanky.

2 Hold the metal end of the kistka above the flame (photo b): not **in** the flame, as this brings soot. Keep it above the flame long enough to get it nice and hot. Then slowly "scoop" out molten wax from the block (photo c). The kistka should be hot enough to melt the wax – *no force is needed*! If it will not melt and scoop wax easily, the kistka is not hot enough. Once the kistka is full (photo d) of molten wax,

Creative Crafts of the World — Pysanky

you can draw with it for a *surprisingly* long time – until it runs dry or cools off to the point where the wax solidifies. Demonstrate for the class how long it writes before it cools too much. **Always** dab the side of the kistka funnel with paper towel after filling it, as it will probably have some stealth molten wax hanging around underneath, just waiting to make a splotch on the unsuspecting egg.

3 Have students practice a few lines on their paper towel to get the feel for it (photo e). Working on the egg will be similar.

4 First, the students should put their initials and the year on the round (bottom) of the egg for later identification (photo f). Moms will thank you, especially if siblings are in your class together. Stress again that the black lines they are drawing with black wax will become *white* lines.

5 At this point, it is a good idea to make "white" division lines on the egg helping the kids to plan the rest of their egg. You can use an egg 'lathe' if you wish (photo g). My students are thrilled with this tool. Divide the surface with horizontal lines freehand or aided by the lathe, which will give stripes, or with vertical lines freehand which will give "orange sections".

6 When all the "white" lines are on their egg, students should carry their treasures to the dye table in their yogurt cup. The only eggs that have broken in my classes (in the hands of the students!) have been crushed or dropped in the excitement of getting to the dye table with an egg in the *hand*. Submerge the egg in yellow dye (photo h). A short dye time will give a pale yellow, but encourage them to leave it longer, as bright colors look the best on the final product.

7 When the egg is bright yellow, remove it and blot it dry on paper towels (photo i). Then give it 5 minutes (or more) to

Creative Crafts of the World — Pysanky

air dry, before the student starts waxing again. I always have the kids make up somewhere between 3 and 5 eggs to keep drying time high for each egg, and also the fact that one could break during the blowing. I remind them of this as the eggs get more and more work invested in them. I've not had many eggs disintegrate during blowing, but when it did happen, no student fell apart since they had been forewarned that it may.

8 Continue drawing "yellow" lines in black wax (photo j). Encourage the students to make small shapes that are filled in with wax – this will give bright spots of yellow on black eggs later and will look great! When all "yellow" black wax lines are drawn, dye in red (photo k).

Once the eggs are dyed in red and dried, the red eggs get wax to cover the parts they want to stay <u>red</u>. If a student wants a large area to stay red (or two paragraphs back, yellow) it is best to scribble thoroughly over the area (photo l). Some have tried dripping wax onto the area, but the thick wax drips are a pain to remove later; picking it off could result in the egg breaking, and trying to melt off that much wax can result in cooked egg!

Draw any motif the student wants to be red, as the heart in photo m.

My best success has been with eggs that are white, yellow, red and black (3 dye

pots). I have been persuaded to have blue and green in there as well, but that's a lot of dye pots, and not all colors completely cover the one before (except black, which covers all). Use your own judgement, but know that white, yellow, red, and black make a dandy egg.

9 At any point, a student can stop with a color that is showing and does not need to finish with black. These are charming eggs, too. Going all the way to black is the traditional way, but let the students create for themselves. I've done many lovely eggs in *one* dye; white egg, decorated all over, dunked in red and done! (photo n) I should mention that a white and yellow egg is not that exciting; not enough contrast.

10 After the second to the last color has been dyed (say, red) and all desired parts have been preserved with wax, the egg goes into the black dye pot (photo o). Dye it long enough to have the egg pitch black. (Please note: after several eggs, the dye bath may become 'exhausted' – make up fresh dye if the eggs come out only grey.)

At this point the eggs are not a pretty sight; all lumpy with wax and black as pitch (photo p). If the lines were done really well (smooth and thin) the egg may show its true colors dimly through the black wax.

11 Now the magic happens: the black wax comes off to reveal all colors at once. Be sure to do this step in front of the class for the 'ooohs' and 'ahhhs'. It can be done a number of ways:

If you have nothing but a candle, a candle works. Hold one part of the egg close to the flame (the *side* of the flame to avoid soot) until the black wax becomes shiny and starts to flow down. Wipe this area with a paper towel and repeat until the wax is gone and the surface is polished.

With a hair dryer you can do a larger area. Be sure to wipe the molten wax right away before it can cool.

An electric embossing tool is like a very hot hair dryer. With a large number of eggs, this tool becomes more useful than dangerous. It makes the wax removal very fast. Be careful with this – only an adult should use it, and I set the egg on a bed of waste rice first (photo q), so as not to have to hold the egg in my hand; even through paper towels this tool can burn your hand! This method goes quickly, but take care not to hold the embossing tool on the egg for more than the *minimum* time necessary; it can cook the egg white, and that makes it challenging to remove later!

12 Spray the wax-free eggs with polyurethane to protect the colors from bleaching during the gutting process (photo r). Allow to dry.

Blowing Out the Shells

13 Once the wax is removed and the eggs have been sealed with polyurethane, it's time to blow the egg guts out. You can do this the old way: a small hole poked with a pin in the top and a larger one in the bottom and blow down and out. Alternatively, the hole can be made with a Dremel (tiny power tool) with a cone-shaped sanding stone (photo s). Make this hole at the top of the egg. This method works a lot better, especially with a large class. It gives a clean, slowly ground hole and almost never cracks the egg.

14 After the hole is bored, use a skinny knitting needle or skewer to puncture the yolk and gently addle the insides for easier blowing (photo t).

15 An egg blow-pipe is the best tool I've found for removing the egg guts. (Yes, I say egg guts – the boys in the class love it!) Using the blow-pipe has the advantage that only one hole needs to be

bored. The kink in the pipe allows the insides to flow out and into a waiting bowl (photo u). Just blow smoothly and with **only** the force needed to start the flow. Alternatively, let an empty 500 ml syringe do the blowing for you and save your lungs.

The colors on the outside of the egg are still water-soluble, and if some goo smears onto the egg, it may remove some of the color if there isn't enough polyurethane.

The guts will be discolored (badly) and should be discarded and **never** consumed. These are not food-grade dyes.

16 A quick rinse with a needle-less syringe full of water using the blowpipe will finish the process.

17 Drain and dry the eggs in egg cartons. Check soon after you place them to make sure the shell was totally empty of water and has not dribbled a puddle that will try to bleach the egg around the bored hole.

18 Findings (photo v) are available to glue on the point end (photo w) of the egg, covering the hole, to hang it if you like.

Afterthoughts

In many countries, "Easter Bushes" are decorated in the home. Pussy-willows, forsythia branches, etc. are placed in a heavy vase, weighted down with marbles if need be, then hung with these charming eggs.

Creative Crafts of the World · Pysanky

81

Dreamcatcher

What better way than this to "protect" little ones from scary dreams? A hand-made symbol of love to hang on their head-board!

History

Today, dream catchers are made by artists from many Native American Nations. However, they are thought to have originated with the Ojibwe from the Great Lakes region (called Chippewa by others). In that culture, articles representing spider webs were hung from the hoop of a child's cradleboard. There, they believed, "they catch and hold everything evil, as a spider's web catches and holds everything that comes into contact with it." (Frances Densmore, *Chippewa Customs*)

New Vocabulary

Polygon: Geometric shape made up of more than three straight sides

Asubakacin: Ojibwe 'white earth band' meaning "net-like, looks like a net"

Bwaajige Ngwaagan: Literally 'curve lake band' in Ojibwe meaning "dream snare"

Materials

- Wooden hoops from embroidery hoop sets (7 inches)
- Web stranding: waxed linen, fishing line, elastic, or simple cotton string
- Scissors
- Superglue
- Beads, charms, crystals, feathers for embellishment
- Binding for hoop: leather cord or bulky yarn
- Large eyed plastic needle

An example made with stretchy bead nylon

Creative Crafts of the World   Dreamcatcher

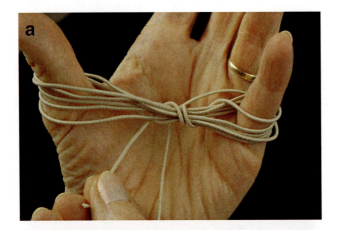

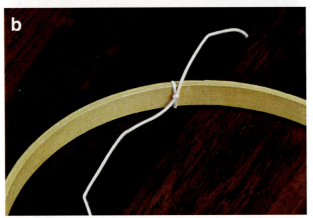

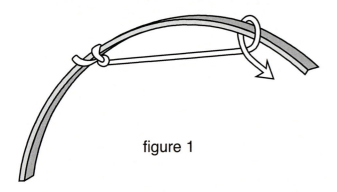

figure 1

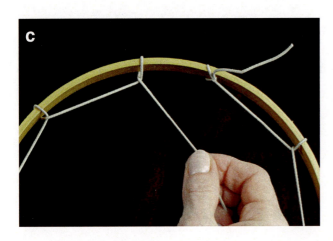

Terminology

<u>Stranding</u>: Yarn, elastic or waxed linen used for making the web

<u>Hoop-binder</u>: Bulky yarn or strips of leather used to cover the wooden hoop

Procedure

1. Cut a piece of web stranding about 4 yards long. This is a lot of length for young ones to handle, but it is best not to have to splice in the middle. The amount of stranding needed will vary according to how the student makes the web; better to have too much than not enough. Wind the length into a butterfly using your hand as a scaffolding (photo a) to make it easier to handle. To make the butterfly: Lay 8 inches of the strand down your forearm and wind the rest of the 4 yards between your thumb and pinky using a figure-8 motion. The last few inches are wound around the middle to from the 'body' of the butterfly. A quick half-hitch holds this end in place. Remove the butterfly from your hand and attach the loose 8 inches to the hoop. As more length is needed it will come smoothly out of the 'wings'. This butterfly will follow the path of the arrowheads in the following graphics.

2. Attach the stranding to the wooden hoop with a double knot, leaving a tail of about 4 inches (photo b) to be embellished later with beads or crystals (or to hide under the hoop-binder). Moving clockwise around the hoop, choose a point to 'attach' the stranding about 1-2 inches from the double knot. Lay the stranding over the hoop and come up from under the hoop <u>behind</u> the 'point of attachment' (figure 1). When tightened in the clock-wise direction, this will form what can be thought of as a half-hitch.

3. Continue 'attaching' the stranding around the hoop until you arrive again an inch short of the double knot (photo

84

c). Take care to keep each of the attachments tight and taut.

4 Starting the second round, the action is the same. You will still use a half-hitch but the point of attachment is now in the middle of the stranding span instead of around the hoop itself (figure 2). Notice that the last half-hitch is being pinched (photo d) to keep it tight and taut while placing the new half-hitch. Watch your students at this point to make sure that they catch every single section with a half-hitch and don't skip one.

The problem that comes up for some students at the beginning of the second round is shown in figure 3. Watch your class carefully because someone *will* forget to do the half-hitch once they are off the wooden hoop.

5 Continue attaching around and around toward the center (photo e).

You will notice that if your hoop has 8 attachment points originally, it will have 8 attachments in every round. They will simply be smaller spans as you approach the center. Now is a great time to talk about geometry and polygons!

6 You can splice in a new color at any time. Tie the new color onto the old strand using a double knot. Leave 6-inch tails of both colors for decoration with beads later.

7 Beads can seem to float in the web if they are strung onto the stranding and left behind as the half-hitches are made. See the photo at end of chapter for examples.

8 There are two choices for finishing the web. It can be closed at a single point, or a circle can be left in the center for a charm. If the student wants to close the web at a *point*, continue looping until the open space forms a small polygon and then he does the 'closing step'. On the other

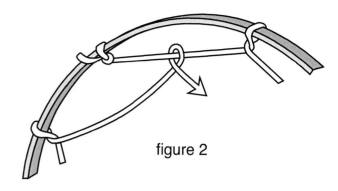

figure 2

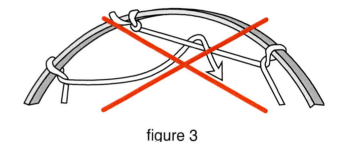

figure 3

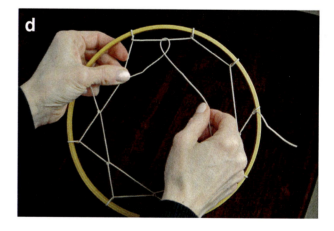

d

e

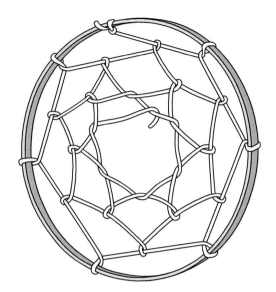

figure 4

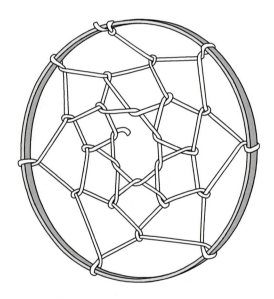

figure 5

hand, if an open hole in the center is desired, he must stop half-hitching well before he is near the center and do the 'closing step'. This results in an open circle in the center of the web and makes a grand frame to hang a favorite charm!

9 In the closing step you will do exactly what you were advised *not* to do while forming the web. You now pass the stranding through each section as shown (and forbidden) above in figure 3. Your hoop will look like figure 4. Pulling the stand tight (figure 5) will give the web a single-point close (photo f). Tie off with two overhand knots and add a dab of superglue, leaving a tail of 6 inches for embellishment if desired.

10 To cover the wooden hoop, take a piece of binder material (I use bulky wool yarn), at a length that is workable. Attach it to the hoop with a double knot leaving a tail. Wind this hoop-binder around and around the wooden hoop being sure to pack the winding together so that all of the wood is covered. Use a plastic needle to make this easier if the space is tight near the hoop. When you get to the attachment points of the stranding, wind nice and close on both sides. This attachment point should become virtually invisible.

Encase all the ends you want to hide (photos g and h)

11 When the hoop is completely wound, hide the end under the winding with a large-eyed needle (photo i).

If using strips of leather as a hoop binder, glue the end in place.

12 If you want, add more embellishment strings elsewhere in the web with a simple double knot. Fill these with beads, feathers, etc. Students can personalize to their heart's content.

Afterthoughts

I have my students bring in things special to them for this class. If you see your students for a full school year, as I do, have them on the look-out for fallen feathers and other bits of nature from September on, and they can use these in this project. This all gives the kids a real personal connection with their finished web. I don't know about stopping nightmares, but these webs do make my students happy!

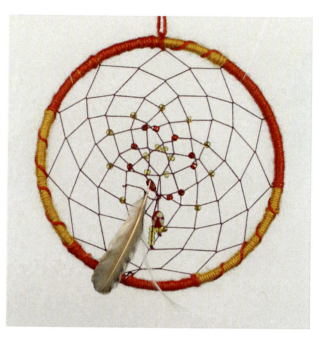

Wet Felting

This craft truly qualifies as magic: loose fibers transform themselves into thick, soft cloth!

History

Felt making is among the oldest cloth-making techniques known to man. One can hardly imagine a more useful gift to early man, than the fact that the wool from the sheep's back can be transformed into cloth without needing to spin and weave the fibers. Already in the early Bronze Age thick, hard, felt caps were being made; decorated for beauty, yet robust enough to be used for protection from blows or sword-cuts. Greek classical literature makes many references to felt use. In Pompeii specialized workshops for felt hat and felt glove production were discovered.

Russian archeologists have found felt pieces in "kurgans", grave sites of Scythians. This ancient nation of horsemen from the 5th century B.C. showed magnificent craftsmanship in felt. Saddle pads, blankets, and many objects for daily use have been found. This skill continues at an impressive level today as seen in the Yurts of Mongolia – portable houses of felt pulled over wooden trellis frames.

Materials

- Table drapes
- Cafeteria trays
- Carded wool for a base batt
- Wool roving in many colors
- Tent (mosquito) netting or plastic screen
- 100% wool yarn bits
- Water cooker
- Large measuring cup - Pyrex 2 to 4 cup
- Murphy's Oil Soap
- Cane placemats
- Stirring spoon
- Rinse buckets
- Vinegar

New vocabulary

<u>Felt</u>: Non-woven cloth produced by 'massive irreversible entanglement' of wool fibers

<u>Staple length</u>: The length of the hair growing on the back of the animal

<u>Carding</u>: Combing cleaned wool fibers to make all fibers lay in the same orientation

<u>Roving</u>: Long snakes of carded wool fiber

<u>Batts</u>: Flat mats of carded wool fiber

<u>Yurt</u>: Round felt houses made by the Mongolians

Felt can also be made around a scaffolding, in this case a very large embroidery hoop

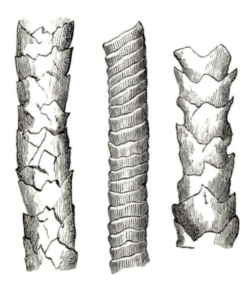

Figure 1

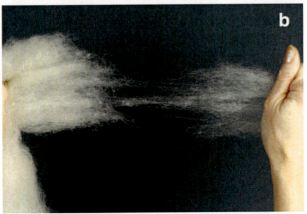

Background

This is how felting works: wool fibers have microscopic "fish scales" on them (figure 1). Under normal circumstances, they lay flush against the fiber shaft. If the wool gets warm, moist and into an alkaline (soapy) environment the scales bloom out. If you then add agitation to the mix, you get massive irreversible entanglement. The mass becomes firm, shrinks and becomes felt. This is exactly why your mom taught you to hand-wash your wool sweaters gently in cold water. Felt is what you get when a wool sweater is added by mistake to a normal laundry load. The adult wool sweater becomes a child's sweater and a child's sweater becomes a doll sweater. Felt happens!

Class Preparation

Protect tables with waterproof table drapes. Each student needs a cafeteria tray or cookie sheet as a work space as well as a piece of plastic netting approximately the size of the tray. Many colors of wool roving should be displayed on a side table along with snippets of 100% wool yarn. Tapestry yarn works well.

When working with wool roving, it is important to note that the roving is *pulled* apart, never *cut*. To do this, grasp the roving with two hands (not too close together) and pull gently. It should flow apart. There are two reasons it may not: first, if your hands are closer together than one staple length you would need to *break* fibers to get them apart. Move your hands farther apart and try again. Typical staple lengths range from 1 to 6 inches. Second, it may be that the roving has felted to itself a bit if it is old roving. To fix this, work the roving wider by opening it up sideways (pull apart at 90° to the direction of the fibers) and try again.

Procedure

For this project a base of background wool is build up and then decorated before felting.

1. To make the best felt, it's important that the wool be laid out in wispy, wispy layers. Grasp the tippy tip ends of the roving (photo a) and pull out one staple length of fiber, thin enough to see through (photo b). This one detail will make the difference between the students having a lumpy felt or a smooth felt. Practice this with them.

2. In this manner, lay out wispy fluffs across the cafeteria tray in a single layer (photo c). Wool felts best when the wispy layers are oriented non-uniformly. Therefore, if your first layer went north-south, the second layer should go east-west.

Continue adding thin wispy layers, alternating directions until the mass stands approximately 5 inches above the tray (photo d). Check that there are no gaps in the mass. These gaps will become holes.

In this way you are offering the wool fibers many chances to 'hold hands and make friends' with many fibers around them which go in different directions.

3. Decorate the top with colored roving (still fluffy and airy!), bits of wool yarn, snippets of wool cloth, etc.

We know that polyester, cotton, linen, mylar strips, plastic, etc. will *not* felt, as they have no scales. That having been said, they can be incorporated into felt in a pinch. If you absolutely want to include a non-feltable element in your piece, lay it on the base

Creative Crafts of the World   Wet Felting

mass and put a layer of wispy feltable wool over the top of it. Many times you can get it to be encapsulated. Better advice when working with kids though; to guarantee success you should use only 100% wool.

Enjoy decorating the white mass. Here the creative spirit of the students can blossom! Cover the mass with the plastic netting (photo e), this will protect the design while the felting process begins.

4   Mix up the soap solution (affectionately known in my classes as glug-glug). Pour 1½ cups of boiling water into a 4-cup Pyrex measuring cup (photo f) and add Murphy's Oil Soap "glug-glug" (this is how I measure it – *very* approximately 3 tablespoons). Stir until the soap is dissolved, then add tap water to bring the level to 4 cups. Use this solution as hot as you can take it, but remember: err on the side of caution when working with kids.

5   Pour a little glug-glug through the screen into the mass (a few tablespoons in many different spots). Don't overdo as you will be amazed how little you can get away with and too much will slosh out of the tray.

6   Press the screen down as the mass gets wet. Its height will collapse to almost nothing (photo g). If some areas still bubble up fluffy, squeeze the liquid through the screen and over to that area from other areas (photo h). Only add more glug-glug if you absolutely cannot wet all areas with the given liquid.

7. Once all is wet, have your kids start rubbing the wet wool through the screen gently at first, being careful not to shift the screen (photo i). Using fingertips apply light to medium pressure at first and have the kids do this for about 2 to 7 minutes. A skin will form on the mass that shows the first sign that the felt is forming (photo j). Once the skin starts to form, you must be careful to avoid including the plastic screen by mistake in the forming of the felt! Lift the screen off and place it on the forming felt again in a slightly different position. Continue rubbing more vigorously now, using your palms or the heels of your hands.

8. Remember to flip the piece over and rub the back in the same way – through the screen.

Often it shows now if you have too much glug-glug. Pour any extra off the tray. Felt happens with *moisture*, not deepwater.

9 There are two ways you can do the edges. Either felt them flat the way they lie (this will give you an uneven, fuzzy but interesting edge) or fold them under (photo k) which will give you a straighter, better defined edge. The edge will still be a little free-form. If the student wants completely straight edges and square corners, have the student felt it to the end, dry the piece completely, and cut it straight with a pair of scissors.

10 Your students continue rubbing until the mass starts to behave like cloth, holding together instead of pulling apart (photo l). This happens probably after 5 to 15 minutes of this more vigorous rubbing.

Turn the piece over and rub on the back for the same amount of time.

11 In order to increase the friction on the now-forming felt, roll it up in a cane placemat (photo m). This is then rolled first with the hands (photo n), then more vigorously with the forearms (photo o). While rolling the piece, stop and change

the orientation of the piece (90 degrees and/or flip it upside down) in the roll every few minutes.

12 Now you can start taking out your aggression on your felt (photo p). Remove the screen for good, scrunch up the felt from the sides, pound it down with your fists, turn it, rub it, pick it up and slam it down onto the tray. This splashes if you had too much glug-glug; pour it off. You can work 5 to 10 minutes more, or longer if you have lots of aggression to work out.

13 Rinse the new masterpiece well in clear water until the soap is out. A quick rinse in dilute vinegar water (¼ cup to 1 gal) will return the wool to the pH it prefers – acidic.

14 Dry flat and enjoy.

Afterthoughts

After this class, the students are very receptive to learn about yurt construction. The Web offers fun videos (see reference page) of the intense process to make the felt for these houses – the rolling stage is done by pulling the huge roll behind a camel or horse!

I have seen these felt pieces done by very young students and be framed to go on the wall as modern art.

Twining

One of the oldest of textile techniques takes on a charming modern project. What treasures will your students hide away in *their* amulet bag?

Creative Crafts of the World — Twining

History

Basket makers across the globe often use twining as a technique in constructing their baskets. The technique can also be used for making cloth, although it is less well-known for cloth-making since it is very labor-intensive with few of the labor-saving tricks we find in weaving. It is formed with only finger manipulation.

But there are examples of twined cloth. The K'iche' women of Zaqualpa, Guatemala for instance use twining on the shoulders of their huipiles (blouses) together with decorative soumak. It is also often used as a finishing technique on rugs before the fringe is tied. Some contemporary rug weavers in the USA also now use this technique to create their entire rugs. (see reference page)

Perhaps the most distinctive garments made using this technique are the amazing Ravenstail robes and Chilkat dancing blankets made for centuries by the Tlingit, Haida, and Tsimshian weavers of the Northwest Coast.

Materials

For the loom:
The loom I use is a simple frame made of ½" PVC plumbing pipe, available in all home maintenance stores. Besides the straight pipe, you will need 2 "L" joints and 4 "T" joints per loom. 4 end-caps on the feet will make the loom stand more stably (photo a, next page).

For each project:
- Wool yarn
- Scissors
- Index cards
- Sharp needles with large eyes
- Beads or coins or other decorations
- Sewing thread

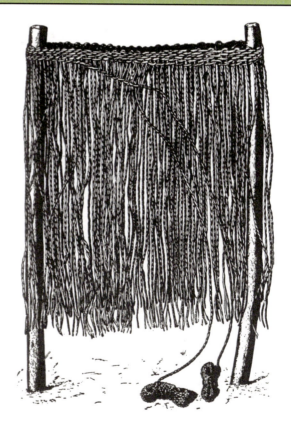

Ojibwe weaving frame
from Clark Wissler, *The American Indian*, 1917

Creative Crafts of the World Twining

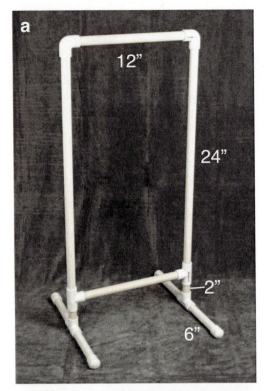

New vocabulary

<u>Warp</u>: Parallel strands on a loom, held in place by gravity

<u>Weft</u>: Strands running perpendicular to the warp threads

<u>Warping board</u>: Convenient frame with prominent pegs used to measure off a number of warp threads

<u>Twine</u>: Weaving method involving crossing two weft threads between each warp thread

<u>Selvage</u>: Two sides of a weaving that do not unravel

Class Preparation

Loom construction

The dimensions of the loom are not critical. A larger loom could be build for a larger project if desired. The loom I use is 12 inches wide and 24 inches tall. Two small connector pieces (2 inches) connect it to the 4 legs (6 inches each). See photo a.

These looms fold flat for storage between school years by rotating the legs.

Procedure

Prepping the warp

1. Cut 10 pieces of yarn 40" long and attach each over the top bar of the loom in a half-hitch. This is made by holding the middle of the yarn as a loop behind the bar (photo b) and bringing both ends through it (photo c). Tug each tight.

2. Push the half-hitches together to make the width less than two inches across. Insert an index card between each of the pairs (photo d). This will be the support you beat *up* against while twining. It may need to be held up until the twining starts, or it may stay in place just fine, if your yarn is 'sticky' enough. If not, a little blue tape will hold it until the twining starts holding it.

Creative Crafts of the World Twining

Twining - the basics

The physical end result of twining is that each pair of weft threads alternate across the warp threads making a cross between each warp thread (see figure e). This can be accomplished in more than one way, but the method that my students have had the most success with is the 'twist' trick.

3 Start with a piece of wool yarn as long as is comfortable for your students to handle. I suggest around a yard. Longer lengths are possible, but there is a trade-off between having to splice less often and having a weft that is so long that it tangles. Fold this weft in half and loop it onto the first warp thread below the index card. Take the two sides of the loop, pinched on either side with your index finger (photo f). Twist the hand 180 degrees (photo g), and place the next warp thread snuggly into the X. Repeat.

You will notice that there are two ways to twist: twisting 'down' (back weft moves over the front weft for the cross) will give you a 'Z' twist to your twining, while twisting 'up' (front weft moves over back weft for the cross) will give 'S' twist.

Twist is an interesting thing. If you twine in one twist direction only (all Z or all S), the cloth will have a lot of accumulated active twist, and will, if you are a tight twiner, actually show torque. This isn't a big problem if the piece is small; it can be controlled when you sew up the sides of the amulet bag. I teach my young students the one-twist-direction way. *This involves turning the loom around each time they get to the end of the row, so that the twining is always performed from left to right.*

If you want the cloth to lay very flat for some reason, say, it is a larger piece, or one that will not be sewn together later, try the two-directions-twist method: one row is twisted 'down' and the return row is twisted 'up' (this can be done with the opposite

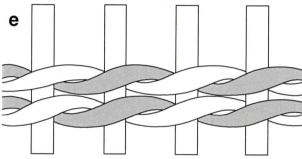

Finger pointing up

Finger pointing down

Twining

hand). This method gives a flat cloth (no active twist, since the twining is balanced) and a pleasing knitted-look texture. *Continue to turn the loom around at the end of each row using this method.*

Twining the Amulet Bag

4 Twine the first row as described on the previous section, being mindful to take one warp thread from the front of the index card and one from the back (photo h). This will lock the card in place. Tighten up the twining (photo i). Continue across the first row (photo j). Once the first row is finished push it up against the card by pushing up on the twining and pulling down on the warp, a few warp threads at a time (photo k).

5 When the student gets to the end of a row of twining and has turned the loom, stress to them that they must twine one cross on the 'outside' of the warp threads, too, before doing the next row (photos l,m). The outside warp threads will show a weft-thread cross between each 2 rows when viewed from the selvage.

6 A technique I use to avoid unwanted draw-in, is to slope slowly downward as I twine the row (photo n). When you get to the end, hold the warp threads firmly with one hand and push the twining row up to lay against the card before turning the loom around.

Splicing in a New Weft

7 At some point, the weft will run out. If the two ends are unequal lengths, the splice must occur when the *first* weft thread runs low. Loop the new weft around a warp together with the last cross of the old (retiring) weft thread (photo o). Leave the old weft hanging, or tuck it in up out of the way into the strings by the index card. At the end of the project, these ends will be hidden with a sharp needle. Continue twining with the new length.

Finishing the Amulet Bag

8 When the fabric is the desired length, open the top bar of the loom to allow the top half-hitches to slide off. Notice that the cloth has torque (photo p). Open these top loops with scissors and hide all warp-ends back into the fabric with a sharp

Creative Crafts of the World   Twining

needle (photo q). The ends being hidden may follow any warp-thread channel but their own. Carefully trim these after hiding them. Also hide all splice ends in the same manner.

9 Twist a number of yarn strands together for the handle, use a fringe twister if desired (photo r), or braid three together. The handle does not *need* to be long enough to go around a person's head – one of my bags has a short little handle and holds the small oil bottle on my spinning wheel.

10 Sew the edges up at the same time you attach the handle with a whip stitch (photo s). Hide all ends into the cloth.

Embellishments

11 Provide beads, coins, charms, etc. for the class to put on their amulet bags. These may be best sewn on with sewing thread, not the wool yarn used for twining. False fringe may be attached (teal bag on following page), but is most easily attached before the bag is sewn closed.

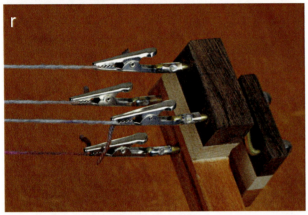

Fringe Twister

Afterthoughts

My students will take three to five 1 hour class periods to do the twining. It takes longer than you would think. If need be, send the looms home with them as homework.

Amulet bags are not the only thing that are nice off this loom. For example, see the trivet below right. This was done with bulky wool yarn, in the S-twist, Z-twist method to make sure it lays flat. Note the 'knitted' texture.

Maasai Beading

This folk craft combines beads and wire to make a stiff little medallion with loads of uses!

History

The Maasai are nomadic cattle herding people in Kenya and northern Tanzania. Cattle alone are wealth in this culture, to the point that one of the most common greetings translates as "I hope your cattle are well".

The Maasai have become known world wide for their dazzling bead work, which they wear with joyful abandon. Both men and women wear jewelry made with beads. The bead colors are typically set in high contrast patterns; dark next to light – reflections of contrasts seen in opposites that occur in natural world (day / night, youth / age, war / peace). Contrast is seen as beautiful and as a natural state.

The colors are significant:

Red: The color of the Maasai

Blue: Godly, reflecting the color of the sky, generosity

White: Peace

Green: The color of God's greatest blessing: fresh grass after a rainfall

The beadwork can be used to identify subgroups, since each group has a dominant color preference.

New Vocabulary

Maasai: An African people found in Kenya and northern Tanzania who are, among many other things, master bead-workers

Terminology

"Leg": One of the four structural wires that will be used to tack the winding wire in place

"Spider": The four wire legs plus the button 'body' that form the skeleton of the medallion.

Materials

- #10 glass beads in primary and secondary colors
- Gauge 24 wire for bead winding
- and for structure
- White buttons with 4 holes
- Wire snips
- Flat beading pliers
- Double round pliers

"Tightening the leg": Grasp and twist the leg wire tight, using double-round needle-nosed pliers.

Creative Crafts of the World   Maasai Beading

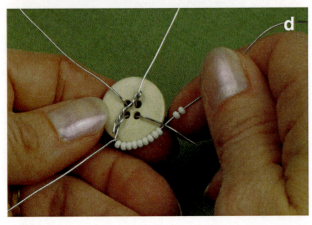

Procedure

1. Choose a design to follow or create your own design. (See end of chapter for examples)

2. Cut 2 strands of gauge 24 "structural" wire and bend them in the middle. Thread each into the 2 opposite holes (photo a) on the button to form the "spider" (photo b).

3. Attach 24" of gauge 24 "spiral" wire on one "leg" near the button by hooking and winding it (photo c). Wind the leg wire once around it to tack it in place (similar to photo e).

4. String on enough beads to reach around the edge of the button to the next spider leg (4 to 12 beads depending on size of button, photo d).

5. Lay the beaded spiral wire along the edge of the button and tack it in place by coiling the leg wire once around it (photo e). Pull the leg wire out straight again.

6. String on another 4 to 12 beads – the number that will fill the space to the 3rd leg wire (photo f) and tack this in place using the 3rd leg wire.

7. Continue in this manner, using increasingly larger bead numbers between leg wires as the arc of the growing medallion gets longer (photo g). Notice that the front of the button is showing in photo g whereas the back was showing in photos e and f. This is why the spiral wire seems to run in the opposite direction in these two photos. The spiral wire will *never* switch directions.

8. Pull the leg wire "tacks" good and tight, using pliers as needed. The trick to a clean-looking medallion is holding the newest beaded arc tightly to the medallion as it is tacked in place (photo h) by each new leg wire wrap. If the student does not

make these tacks tight, the medallion will look loose and untidy (photo i).

9 To splice in a new spiral wire, end the old wire by hooking it around the leg wire it reaches last (photo j). Clamp it tightly and clip it real close (¼" or less) with wire snips. Hook and clamp a **new** wire tightly (with needle nosed pliers) around the last

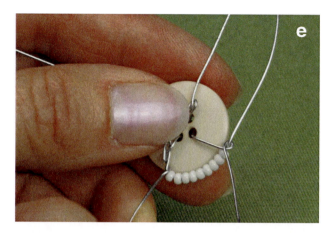

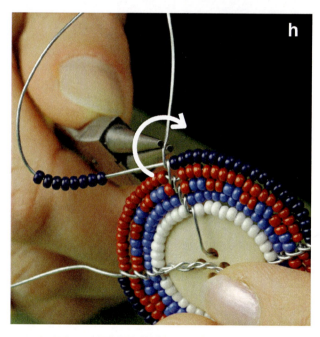

Creative Crafts of the World — Maasai Beading

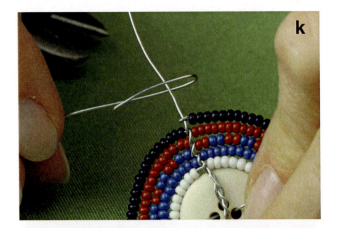

k

l

m

n

spiral wire (photo k) and continue threading beads on as before.

10 For patterned medallions, say an expanding V of new color, I have found it best to string on the beads and test-lay them (photo l) to see how they will fit with a pattern rather than map out the pattern on paper and string-on following *only* the number of beads. The bead width itself can vary greatly and this may mess up any great pattern plan. Best to "go with the flow" and make adjustments to the plan as needed.

Finishing the Medallion

11 When the medallion is large enough, the leg wires must be secured and trimmed (photo m). Bend the leg wire towards the back and trim off short (photo n).

12 The spiral wire can be used to make a hanging loop before it is ended. String on 10-12 beads (photo o) and instead of progressing to the next leg wire, loop it through the spot it is attached, forming a loop (photo p). Secure the wire and snip off close. Needle nose pliers help push ends away from where they would poke sensitive skin.

13 Between classes keep the students' projects in a bouquet to keep them under control (photo q).

Afterthoughts

Besides the obvious uses of pendents or earrings, these medallions if made robustly make great folky zipper-pulls for students' backpacks.

Creative Crafts of the World

Maasai Beading

Bow Loom Weaving

I've been teaching this little project to home school co-op kids for years. It's easy as pie and a grand introduction into weaving for children.

Creative Crafts of the World — Bow Loom Weaving

History

This "primitive " loom is used in North-West Thailand by the Akha people to make narrow bands with beaded selvages that are then used as chin straps and borders for the elaborate hats of their traditional costume. These bands are also applied as decoration to jackets and bags.

New Vocabulary

Warp: Threads on a loom that are held under tension and parallel

Weft: Threads in a weaving that are inserted perpendicular to the warp threads

Shuttle: Device used to hold weft thread and ease its insertion into the warp threads

Selvage: The right- and left edges of a woven fabric, lying parallel to the warp

Pick: One pass of the weft thread

Materials

For each loom:
- One 4' long ¼" dowel or young stalk of bamboo
- 4 heavy-duty paperclips
- Duct tape
- Stiff sponge
- Tapestry needle (dull) for a shuttle

For each student:
- Yarn for warp and weft, 3/2 or 5/2 Pearl Cotton works best
- GUM brand dental floss threader
- #6 glass beads (200 count)
- Scissors
- Sharp Needles for hiding ends

Class Preparation: Building the Loom

- Open 2 sturdy paperclips to an "S" shape and duct tape one of them at each end of the dowel with just a bit peeking out (photo a). This is the "eye" where you will attach the warp.
- Try to get both "eyes" on the top plane of the dowel (as it's lying on the table). It isn't critical, but there will be less twisting of the warp threads if both eyes are in the same plane.

Procedure

Prepping the warps

1. I would suggest you, the teacher, weave a band yourself before bringing this project to the students. First, choose a color of warp thread and cut 5 individual warp threads the length of the dowel. Make an overhand knot about 1" from the end. This is now the top of your warp.

2. Choose any 2 of the 5 warp threads (it doesn't matter which ones) and, using the GUM dental floss threader as a needle, string 100 beads onto each of these 2 warps (photo b). The beaded warps will become the selvages of the band and the 3 inside warp threads will be the weft-faced plain weave warps. It is very important to tie slip knots into the *beaded* warps before you pick the bundle up, or you may have to start over. This is especially important to stress when teaching your students – 200 beads hitting the floor make a very sad sound.

3. Open another paperclip to an S shape and tie the top of the warp bundle to it with a double knot and hook it into the top eye of the loom (photo c).

Stringing the bow

4. To string up the bow, a knot is now placed about an inch from the bottom of the warp, but take care; the warps should be the same length before the knot goes in. The beaded warps are heavier and will *sag* and therefore be longer (photo d). You do not want this. This is critical, and here you should watch your young weavers closely. Pull these slackers tight (photo e) before you untie the 2 slip knots and tie the

Creative Crafts of the World — Bow Loom Weaving

bottom knot. The bottom knot is a double knot tied around the last paperclip.

5. Grasp the end of the bow firmly in one hand and gently pull the warp bundle toward you (photo f). The dowel will bend surprisingly well without breaking. This having been said, in classes I lose about one bow in 20 (just from imperfections in the wood, I assume). Be careful as you bend it in case yours is one that wants to snap. Once you hook the bottom paperclip into the bottom eye, check the tension. You should be able to "bounce" your hand on the warps. If it is "mushy", un-string the bow, tie a new double knot for the bottom paperclip farther up, and re-string.

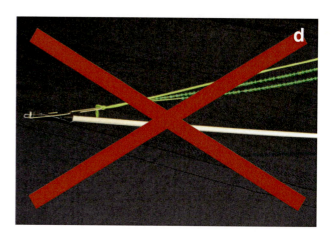

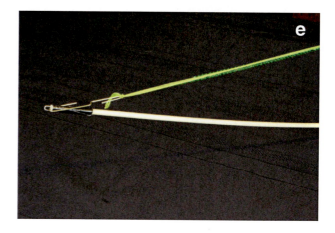

Placing the "Bridge"

6. I have designed a spacer for the bow loom to aid in weaving. I use a piece of stiff sponge, about 2" x 1" shaped like this:

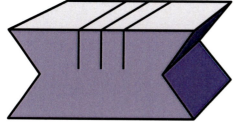

The "hour-glass" sides hold the beaded warps (and hold the beads up out of the way!) and the slots in the top hold each of the three inner warps (photo g).

The bridge – so named because it looks like the bridge on my son's violin – helps keep the warps visible and tidy during weaving.

The bridge also affects the *width* of the weaving: while weaving the beginning triangle, I keep the bridge close and this encourages the

warps to spread out to weaving width. It is important, though, once the weaving is under way, to move the bridge as far up the warp as possible or the band will want to get ever wider.

Weaving

7 The "beginning triangle" is woven first. Thread about 1 yd. of weft thread through a tapestry needle and tie the end around all 5 warp threads (about ⅓ of the way up the warp) leaving a tail. The tail will be hidden with a sharp needle after the weaving is finished.

8 Start weaving plain weave (over under, over under) across all 5 warps (photo h). Beat the picks in, using either the needle or the weft itself. Tight and frequent packing will give a tidy band. The width will increase over 5-10 picks to the width the band "wants" to be woven at.

9 Once you are weaving at width, prepare for the first 2 beads by weaving plain weave on **only** the inner 3 warps until the packed picks reach the height of a bead (photo i).

Slide one bead from each side into the space you have already prepared for them. Weave across all 5 warps once to lock in the beads (photo j).

Be sure to move the bridge far away, up the warp, to keep it from splaying your selvages.

10 Repeat in this fashion (photo k): weave on **only** the inner 3 warps to the height of one bead. Then slide 1 bead from each side into place and lock them by weaving across all 5 warps. Do this until all beads are used up.

Splicing in a new weft

11 Always place the splice where the weaving action is across all 5 warps (between beads). Cut the weft that is ending to a couple inches, and leave it hanging.

Come in from the opposite side with a new weft on the needle (photo l) and follow the ending weft's path exactly (2 passes of the weft in one shed; one is retiring and one is being born). Pull in until the new tail is also a couple inches, and you have tails hanging out on opposite sides of the band.

Continue weaving as normal (photo m). Once the band is done, hide the tails in the weave with a sharp needle. I usually need

Creative Crafts of the World   Bow Loom Weaving

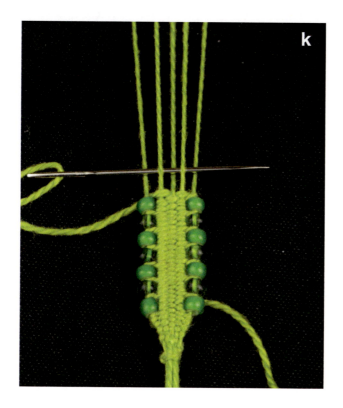

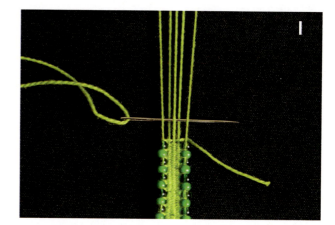

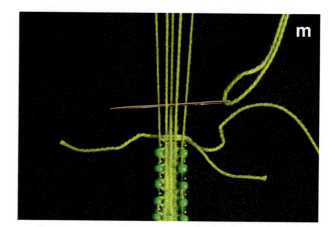

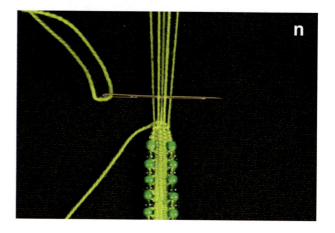

to splice about every 2 inches along the band.

Finishing

12 The "finishing triangle" is woven across all 5 warps, pulling each pick gradually tighter (photo n), taking care to match the pitch of the starting triangle, until the warps are tight together. Two half-hitches will bind them together for good. Thread the weft onto a sharp needle to hide the tail in the weave.

Variations

You can place more than 1 weft pass between the bead pairs. You can weave for an inch between beads if you wish!

Or try using a different number of warp threads. Four is the minimum – yes, an even number! It works, try it!

Many other variations can be achieved by changing the weight of the weft. Fine wefts yield fine bands, change the size of the beads accordingly. (see photo o)

Afterthoughts

For those students who want a more 'natural' loom, narrow bamboo can be used instead of dowels. (See title picture of this chapter). For this you need only *two* paperclips per loom because they can be hooked directly into the bamboo.

The bands can be used as headbands, hat bands, choker necklaces, bracelets, garment embellishments, or whatever the kids come up with: handles for cell phone cases… the possibilities are endless!

Creative Crafts of the World — Bow Loom Weaving

Three possible weaving positions

Dragon Boats

Oh my, are these ever fun to make! With this craft, students watch with delight to see common cardboard magically transform into a small jewel.

Creative Crafts of the World — Dragon Boats

History

In China, the Dragon Boat Festival on the fifth day of the fifth month (Lunar Calendar) is a big celebration, called 'Double Fifth'. Boats are raced, powered by young rowers and cheered on by the people on the shore.

As the day approaches, ladies in the neighborhoods prepare the traditional dragon boat sachets. The sachet is made of colorful cloth or ribbon and stuffed with perfume or herbal medicines. These small gifts will be given out to neighbors during the festival.

New Vocabulary

<u>Triangular bi-pyramid</u>: The shape of the dragon boat sachets, two pyramids with triangular bases joined together

<u>Vertex</u>: A point where three (or more) lines come together

Terminology

<u>Face</u>: One flat side of the bi-pyramid

<u>Points</u>: Corners of the bi-pyramid where the glass headed pins are placed

Materials
- Sturdy, non-corrugated cardboard
- Box cutter
- Cutting mat
- Metal or hard plastic straight edge for cutting and scoring
- Scotch tape
- Narrow ribbon or Perle cotton thread
- Small tassels
- Tacky glue
- Scissors
- Large headed pins (many colors) for corners

<u>Top</u>: Corner of the bi-pyramid where the loop is placed

<u>Bottom</u>: Corner of the bi-pyramid where the tassel is placed

Variegated Ribbon

Patterned Ribbon

Creative Crafts of the World — Dragon Boats

Class Preparation

I bring 2" x 6" blanks pre-cut to the class. If you have young students, you will probably want to do the scoring step yourself ahead of time, as well. My middle-schoolers and older have no trouble with the scoring step.

Procedure

1. Have cardboard blanks cut for the students exactly 2" x 6"

2. Score the cardboard blanks along the lines shown in figure 1 (photo a). Score about half way through the cardboard. We want a very clean fold here, but want it to hold together, too.

3. Bend each of the 5 score-lines cleanly over a hard edge (photo b).

4. The cardboard base will naturally fold together into the required shape, but before you tape it closed, place the loop (photo c) and the tassel in their places. Please note, their places are the vertex where NO diagonal line arrives. They are taped hanging **out** of the cardboard shape, as seen in photo d.

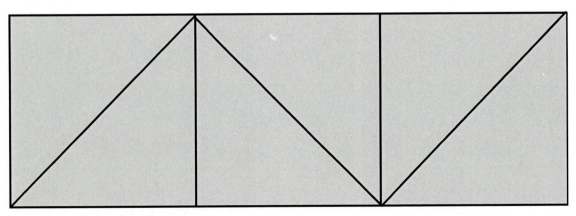

Figure 1

5. Fold up the bi-pyramid and tape the edges securely. Attention to crisp points and close attachments (photo e) will give the best result. That having been said, if the tassel is on a thick cord, you will always have some gapping. This will not be a problem in the finished product.

6. At the three points on the 'sides' of the bi-pyramid, dab tacky glue and force in one glass-headed pin per point (photo f). The glue will hold the pin a bit more securely than just the cardboard alone. Plus, a bit of tacky glue holding the edge of the first row of ribbon winding doesn't hurt either!

The three pins in the photographs are red, green, and blue (photo g) in order to better show the orientation of the bi-pyramid during the winding. The student's dragon boats will most likely have all three pins the same color.

The winding is very simple – once the first round is accomplished! The students will need instruction to get the first round right; after that they will be off to the races!

7. Tape the end of the ribbon to the edge of the bi-pyramid on the left-hand face heading up towards the loop as seen in

Figure 2: View from the top

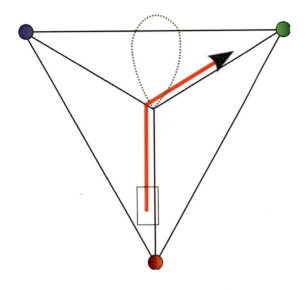

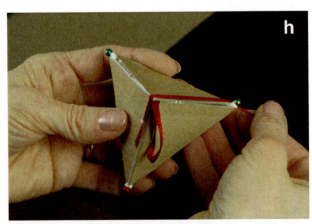

figure 2. At the top, turn the corner and head back down towards the green pin. You have laid ribbon on 2 faces (photo h). Keep the ribbon taut.

8. At the green pin head, swing the ribbon hard around in a 180 degree turn (laying it strategically into any excess glue) and re-orient the bi-pyramid with the green pin down. Now do exactly what you did for step 7; lay the ribbon up the side of the left face heading toward the loop. At the top, turn the corner and head down toward the blue pin. You have laid ribbon on 2 faces (photo i). Keep the ribbon taut. Lay the ribbon in the glue surrounding the blue pin.

Watch out for this problem: sometimes students will lay the ribbon from pin to pin. Never do this! The ribbon must go from a pin to the loop, down to the next pin, and back to the loop.

9. The same now for the blue pin; re-orient the blue pin down and wind across 2 faces towards the red pin (photo j), laying the ribbon in the glue and returning to the beginning of the ribbon. Cover the beginning of the ribbon (photo k), and continue laying the ribbon of the second round along the left side of the ribbon in round one (photo l). Always scoot the ribbon you are laying right up-close and personal to the ribbon already there.

10. Following this path, the bi-pyramid will slowly, magically transform (photos m and n). The winding will start moving down away from the loop, and will eventually end up enclosing the whole bi-pyramid ending at the tassel!

Check to see that the students are keeping the edges butted-up right next to the row before. If cardboard is showing through (photo o) anywhere, move the rounds of ribbon to touch (photo p).

Continue winding (photo q).

Creative Crafts of the World   Dragon Boats

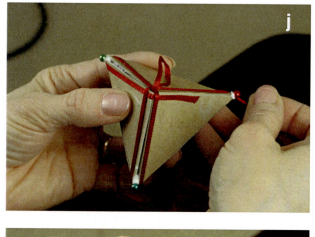

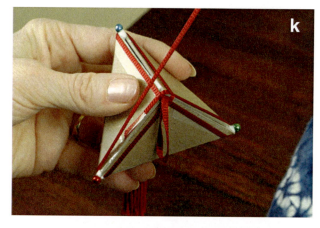

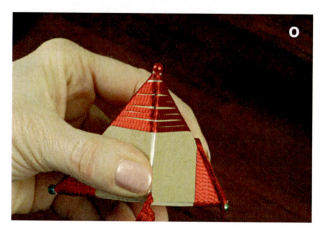

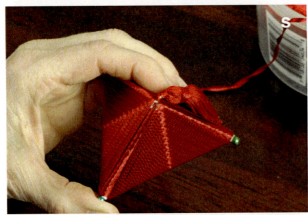

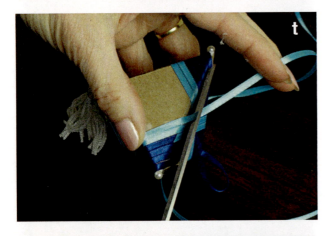

11 As the last of the cardboard disappears under the ribbon, add a dab of glue (photo r) and lay the ribbon into it. Hold it under firm tension until dry enough to snip off flush with the surface (photo s).

I suggest the first bi-pyramid the students wind be a one-color design. Once they have the winding technique down, however, lots of fun variations are available!

12 To introduce a second color, glue and snip the first ribbon out (photo t). Glue again and introduce a new color (photo u) – but be sure to wait until this join is dry enough to handle the tension it will face as the ribbon is wound on tight and taut. Join at the horizontal edge. If this join is done soon after the beginning of the winding (photo v), the join will be covered completely and disappear magically.

Two strands can be wound simultaneously. Watch that they do not get crossed (photos w,x).

3/2 perle cotton can be used as winder (photo y). This takes longer, since it is narrower, but the colors available make it worth the time!

Creative Crafts of the World — Dragon Boats

Afterthoughts

The original use of these decorations was as a sachet. Ambitious students can fill the shapes with lavender for dragon boats to hang with the woolens in the summer to ward off moths. Dragon boats also look fantastic on the Christmas tree, and as always, grandmas, teachers, and parents love to get these as gifts!

w

x

y

For your Inspiration

Block Printing – Nepal

Artist: Christine Lewis

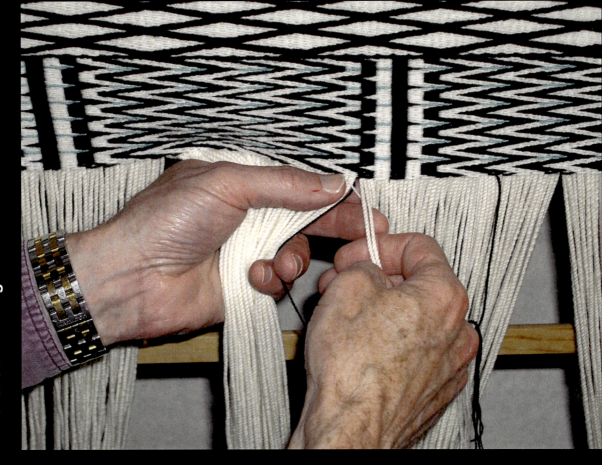

Ravenstail Twining

Huichol Beaded Gourd

Chinchero Weaving & Natural Dyes

Weaver: Santusa Huamán Pumayalli
The Center for Traditional Textiles of Cusco

Afghanistan Wet Felting

Maasai Beading

Artist: Kirsinyinye Parantai; Photo by Moses Kinayia

Bavarian Baumschmuck

unsigned

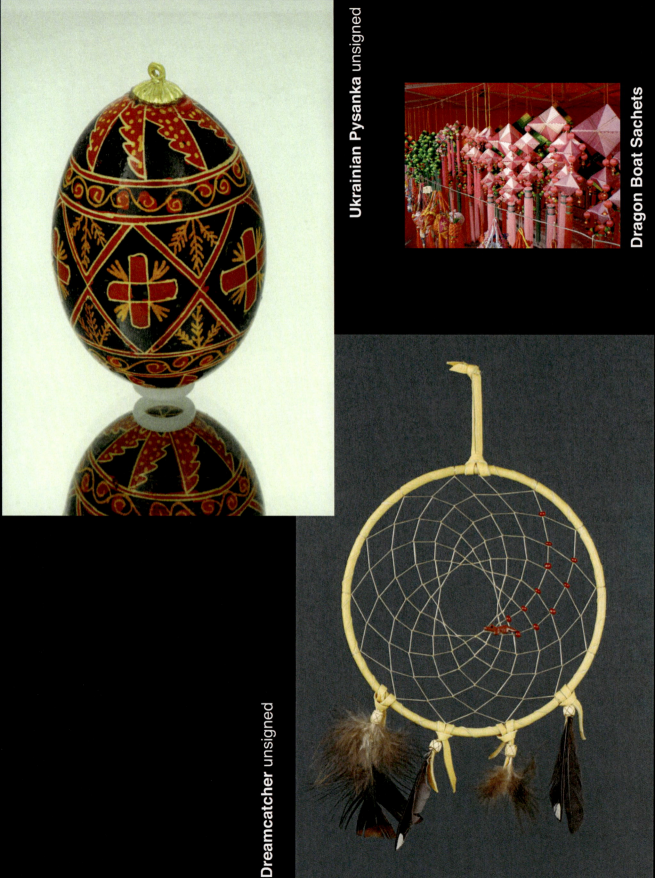

Ukrainian Pysanka unsigned

Dragon Boat Sachets

Dreamcatcher unsigned

Appendix A: Aboriginal Dot Painting Outlines and Symbols

The outlines are also available for you at www.taprootfolkarts.com/ccwbook/dotpaintoutline. This web page uses a format for the drawings that allows you to scale it to any desired size.

Creative Crafts of the World

Appendix A: Outlines and Symbols for Aboriginal Dot Painting

Creative Crafts of the World Appendix A: Outlines and Symbols for Aboriginal Dot Painting

Creative Crafts of the World   Appendix A: Outlines and Symbols for Aboriginal Dot Painting

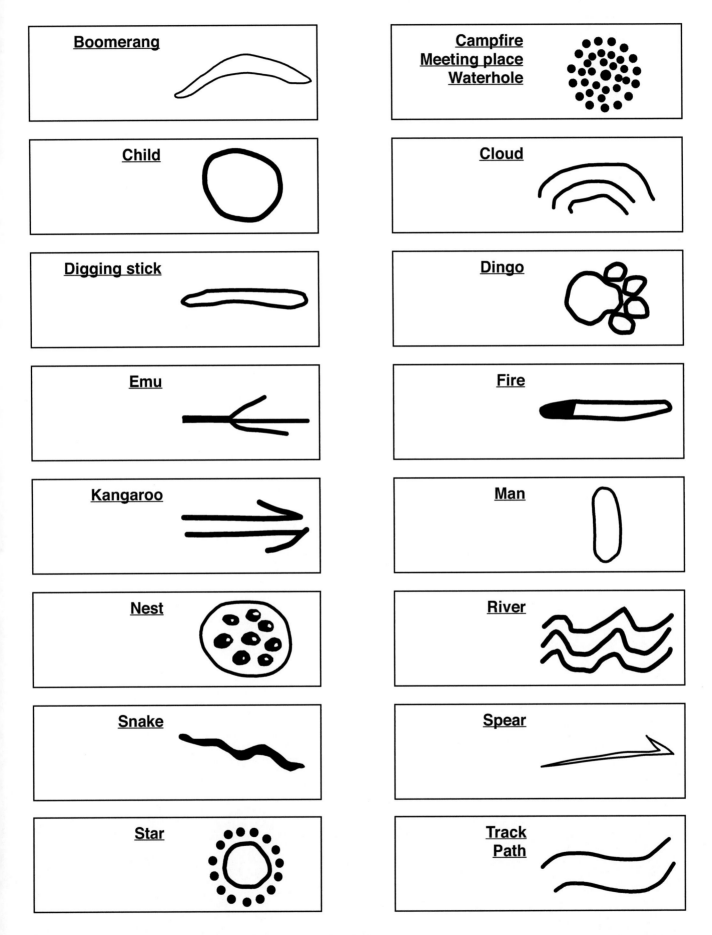

Creative Crafts of the World   Appendix A: Outlines and Symbols for Aboriginal Dot Painting

Tracks

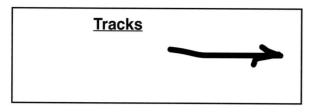

**Woman
People sitting**

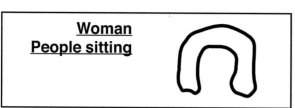

People around camp

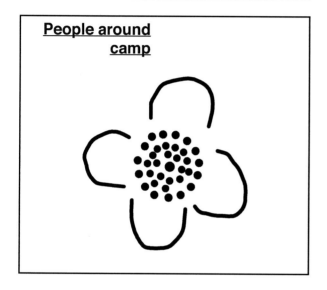

Traveling signs

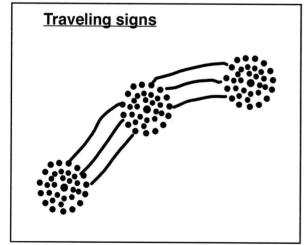

**Water
Smoke**

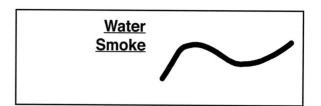

Rain

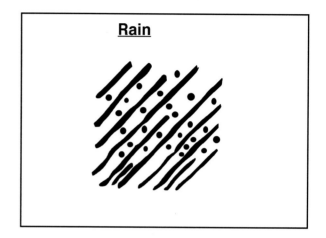

Connected water holes

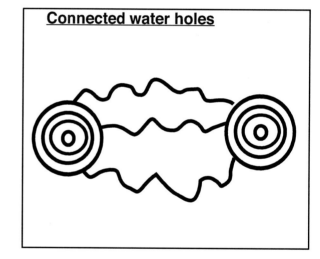

Appendix B: Symbols for Pysanky

Ribbons
everlasting life, and water

Net, Sieve
Christ's reference to becoming "fishers of people", separating good and evil

Dots
stars, Mary's tears while Jesus was on the cross

Fish
ancient symbol for Christ

Crosses
Christ, or the Four Corners of the World

Triangles or little baskets
Holy Trinity, knowledge

Pine needles
health, stamina, eternal youth

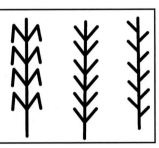

Rose, 8 pointed star
love, caring, success, ancient symbol for Christ

Butterfly
symbol of resurrection

Creative Crafts of the World | Appendix B: Symbols for Pysanky

Deer, Horses
wealth, prosperity, endurance, speed

Birds
fertility and fulfillment of wishes, spring, good harvest
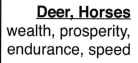

Sun
life, warmth, fortune, growth, eternal existence of God

Windmill
happiness

Rake
agriculture

Flower
female, elegance, beauty, children

Church
Christian faith, house of worship

Ram's horn
masculine, leadership, creativity

Ladder
prosperity, prayer
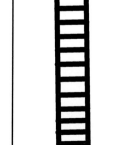

Wheat
bountiful harvest

Appendix C: Resources

Aboriginal Dot Painting

I get my paper at the local craft store, Michael's, JoAnn, or Ben Franklin. Any scrapbooking store will carry lovely 12" x 12" paper.

Acrylic paint is also available from the local craft stores. Q-tips I get at the grocery store.

Recommended Books:

The Inspired Dream: Life as Art in Aboriginal Australia Editor Margie K.C. West ISBN 0730 700 216

Icons of the Desert: Early Aboriginal Paintings of Papunya (Herbert F. Johnson Museum of Art) ISBN 10 : 1934260061

Aboriginal Designs Penny Brown ISBN 978-1-84448-253-5 This is a wonderful book for the teacher! It contains simple outlines of many motifs for the student to copy.

Web sites about the paintings:

- http://en.wikipedia.org/wiki/Indigenous_Australian_art
- http://www.tribalworks.com/aboriginal_art_dot_painting_gallery.htm
- http://www.aboriginalartstore.com.au/aboriginal-art-culture/aboriginal-dot-paintings.php

YouTube has many exciting videos about Dot Painting:

- http://www.youtube.com/watch?v=v-0HYOepu6g This is my favorite
- http://www.youtube.com/watch?v=vQgpHxGVd4Q This may be a bit long to show your kids all of it (13 minutes!) but show them some scenes.

About Dreamtime stories:

- http://www.teachers.ash.org.au/jmresources/dreaming/stories.html
- http://www.janesoceania.com/australia_aboriginal_dreamtime/index1.htm

---

Viking Knitting

I get my wire and tools at the local craft store, Michael's JoAnn, or Ben Franklin. Dowels I get at the home improvement store. Draw plates can be made for the class by the instructor if you have access to wood-working tools, but can also be purchased online; Google for 'Viking Knitting draw plate for purchase'

If your students enjoy Viking Knitting, suggest that they explore the world of chain-mail too.

Video:

Beaded Viking Knit Bracelet featuring Denise Peck ISBN 978-1-59668-151-4

Huichol Beading

Pronunciation guide:

Huichol: Wee-**chohl**

I buy my beads for any of my crafts not at the local craft store, where the bead quality is questionable – specifically the *height* of the beads can vary widely – but rather from a specialty bead store. I use Shipwreck Beads out here in the Northwest (http://www.shipwreckbeads.com/) and have good experience with them through the mail.

Coconut half-shells are available for purchase on the web, sanded, un-sanded, polished, even with a base for secure standing! My advice is to avoid the ones that are deep, the kids have a hard time laying the beads up under the lip. Open and fairly flat works best. Wooden eggs for bases as well as Tacky Glue are purchased at the local craft store, Michael's, JoAnn's, or Ben Franklins.

YouTube has some very nice videos on the technique:

- http://www.youtube.com/watch?v=cyTgurhGUk
- http://www.youtube.com/watch?v=2zjNu-aF5Ak
- http://www.youtube.com/watch?v=bgtfTN7R8_0   *This one is must see!*

If you Google for images of Huichol Beading, you will wow your class. Some of these pieces give me shivers they are so lovely.

Natural Dyes

The thrift store sees a lot of me buying equipment; crock pots, spoons, salad spinners. Once I have dyed with it, it is not to be used again for food preparation, so why not pay as little as possible? Since I teach these classes again each year, the investment in the equipment (however frugal) is a good one.

Onion skins, turmeric, blackberries and black tea bags, alum and cream of tartar are all available at the grocery store. Other leaves and bark are available in your back yard!

Black walnut hulls are available from many of your neighbors, or if not, I can sell you some of mine. Contact me via my web site for price and availability.

100% wool yarn for dyeing is available at your local craft or yarn store, or of course off the web. Here's another tip, I teach the kids to spin wool into yarn with drop spindles and spinning wheels (not covered in this book but a dandy skill to teach kids!) before the Natural Dye unit and they can dye the yarn they have *made*.

A *great* place for further study is Earthhues here in Seattle or at http://www.earthues.com/ Anything you want to learn about natural dyes, they will teach you, plus they sell color extracts, raw dyestuffs, mordants, educational materials, as well as offering classes. Check them out!

Books:

Wild Color by Jenny Dean, 1999, published by Watson-Guptill Publications
ISBN 0-8230-5727-5

This is my favorite natural dye book! There is also a revised edition of this book. Even if you don't use all the great plants and ideas in the book, it's worth having to show your students the colors that are out there.

Weaving

Thick foam board is available at sign shops (e.g. Kinko's), or wood is from the local home improvement store, where you can also get duct tape and paint stir-sticks. Use bulky weight yarn for warp – wool works best, as it tends to 'hold hands' a bit with its neighbors. The weft can be anything, but with elementary kids, use Lamb's pride brand. It's bulky and comes in *great* colors. Do not use Lamb's Pride brand for the warp, it is not plied and is not robust enough to use as warp with kids, Get the yarns at your local yarn store (I shop at The Weaving Works here in Seattle www.weavingworks.com) or at http://www.brownsheep.com

Books:

This is where I got the design for the board-loom:

Small Loom and free-form Weaving by Barbara Matthiessen, 2008 published by Creative Publishing international, Inc. ISBN 1-58923-361-1

If some of your students are interested in pursuing weaving as a skill, I heartily recommend:

Learning to Weave by Deborah Chandler, 1995 published by Interweave press, Inc.
ISBN 1-883010-03-9

If some of your students are interested in the whole loom-thing, this is a fascinating book on the history of looms:

The Book of Looms by Eric Broudy, 1979 published by University press of New England
ISBN 0-87451-649-8

Baumschmuck

Pronunciation Guide:

- Baumschmuck: **bahoom**-shmuk (bahoom- semi-rhymes with 'town', -schmuk rhymes with 'look'
- Tannenbaum: **tahn**-nehn-bahoom
- Christbaum: **krist**-bahoom (krist- rhymes with 'list')

Wooden rounds and cording for the outside are both available at your local craft store, Michael's, JoAnn, or Ben Franklin. Seeds and spices are from the grocery store. Don't forget about the free sources too – look for small acorns and tiny pine cones in your neighborhood!

Of course, you know I'm going to recommend a trip to Bavaria to see more of these little gems! *Christkindlmärkte* (Christmas Markets) are set up in each town during Advent (the four Sundays before Christmas Day) in the town- or village-square. Get a warm mug of *Glühwein* (mulled wine) to drink, or a hand-made *Lebkuchen* cookie to enjoy while browsing the little huts offering Christmas wares.

Paper Stars

Drachenpapier paper is a heavy-duty waxed paper in a rainbow of colors, and comes in large sheets to be used in a variety of crafts (stained-glass windows made of this and construction paper are really cool!) It is available throughout Europe, buy a mailing tube from the paper shop at the same time to get the large sheets home without creasing in your suitcase! Less fun than a trip to Europe, but much more practical in the USA, you can order it through Nova Natural Toys and Crafts (http://www.novanatural.com) where it is listed under 'paper crafts' and is referred to as 'transparency paper'.

Web sites:

- http://www.basteln-gestalten.de/weihnachtsstern
- http://korona81.wordpress.com/tag/transparentpapier/ You don't need any German, just follow the pictures
- http://www.wunderkessel.de/forum/hobbys/32977-transparentpapier-stern-basteln.html Click on the thumbnails to see the photos much better.

Block Printing

I get my Fun Foam and my Tulip brand fabric paint at the local craft store; Michael's, JoAnn, or Ben Franklin's. Here they also sell ready-made foam printing blocks meant for printing on walls, I believe.

My wooden blocks I get from local flooring stores – I relieve them of their old out-of-date hardwood flooring samples. Reduce, Reuse, Recycle! Of course, you can also saw up 1x4s from the home improvement store as well.

Block Printing is a fun one to look up on YouTube! You can find videos of craftsmen in India carving (!) the ones they use, as well as printing with them.

The web offers lovely carved wooden blocks for purchase – some from India and Pakistan – a few examples of these can add a lot to a lesson.

- http://www.youtube.com/watch?v=0-qLUPW4KfI *This is a must-see!*
- http://www.youtube.com/watch?v=6-HTv0gR5Ns Good example of newspaper placement

Pysanky

Pronunciation Guide:

Pysanky: **Pis**-ahn-kee (pis- rhymes with 'this', -kee rhymes with 'knee')

Kistka: **keest**-kah (keest- rhymes with 'least')

Virtually everything you need for this class except the eggs themselves are found at The Ukrainian Gift Shop.(http://www.ukrainiangiftshop.com) They have kistkas, black (and yellow) wax, design suggestions, dyes, gut-blowing pipes, findings for hanging, even display stands and finished Pysanky for you to show your class (Oh, are these lovely!).

An alternative is Pysanky USA. (http://www.pysankyusa.com)

Embossing tools for really hot air are sold in scrap booking stores or any local craft store. E6000 glue is also available at craft stores.

Dremel tools for boring holes in the egg shells are available from home improvement stores. You will also need the conical sandstone attachment.

Books:

Ukrainian Easter Eggs And How We Make Them by Kmit, Luciow & Perchyshyn
ISBN 0-9602502-0-4

YouTube:

- http://www.youtube.com/watch?v=MzVicHadJfc   *This is a must-see!*

Dream Catcher

I use the circle half of a 7" wooden embroidery hoop from the local craft store as a base. (The split half I discard). Elastic cord, cotton thread, elastic beading strand, and decorative beads also come from a Michael's, JoAnn, or Ben Franklin. Don't forget to use the found objects the kids bring in.

Feathers are available at http://www.zuckerfeathers.com

YouTube:

- http://www.youtube.com/watch?v=AJMEAIW6B8o
- http://www.youtube.com/watch?v=H7HvcgFqFIU Three legends told

Book referenced:

Densmore, Frances (1929) *Chippewa Customs*. St.Paul: Minnesota Historical Society Press

Wet Felt

Wool roving is not something that is available in reasonable amounts in your local craft store. Your city may have a fiber-arts store, or you can order it off the Web. These companies are very good:

- http://weavingworks.com Under yarns and fibers, click fibers, and the New Zealand Corriedale will come up. Click on the pink roving bump and all the available colors will show!
- http://halcyonyarn.com/fibers/fiberswildwooly.html

Mosquito netting comes from camping stores, Murphy's oil soap is in the grocery store.

YouTube:

- http://www.youtube.com/watch?v=gJ0uojUHYdA *This is a must see!* Felt-making in Mongolia
- http://www.youtube.com/watch?v=VeDsIWfV9tE Though certainly more elaborate than most, this shows some very nice yurt decoration.

Books:

Felt: New Directions for an Ancient Craft by Gunilla Paetau Sjöberg ISBN 1-883010-17-9 This one is my favorite because of the history, the pictures, and the cultural background it gives. On top of this, it even has projects!

Chapter graphic:

The Chemistry of Hat Manufacturing, lecture by Watson Smith delivered to the Hat Manufacture's Association, 1906 (http://www.gutenberg.org/files/17740/17740-h/17740-h.htm)

Round Llama felt by Shelly Vollstedt (page 89)

Twining

½ inch PCV piping for the single bar loom is purchased at the home improvement store. I don't even glue the pieces together, although you could.

Any worsted weight yarn works for this craft, personally I prefer 100% wool. The eye-popping yarn used in the title page photo for this chapter was spaced-dyed by hand by Janis Thompson (http://www.dyelots.com). The fine variegation of this yarn is what gives the amulet bag a look of tapestry.

Books:

- *Twined Rag Rugs* by Bobbie Irwin ISBN 0-87341-898-0 A great resource for further study!
- *Twist & Twine* by Bobbie Irwin ISBN 978-0-89689-736-6 Ditto!

Web site on Ravenstail:

- http://www.uas.alaska.edu/soundings/archive-files/2007/04-13/weaving.html

Chapter graphic:

- Wissler, Clark (1917) *The American Indian.* New York: Douglas C. McMurtrie

---

Maasai Beading

Pronunciation Guide

    Maasai: mah-**sahee** (-sahee rhymes with 'fry')

I purchase beads for this craft not at the local craft store, but at a specialized bead shop, my experience is the beads are more uniform. The wire can come from the craft store, as can the tools.

Most everyone has a jar of buttons, or they can be purchased at any sewing shop.

YouTube:

- http://www.youtube.com/watch?v=wv4DgNIuEiM A lovely montage of photographs

---

Bow Loom Weaving

You will be more satisfied with the beads purchased at a specialized bead shop for this craft. The heights of the beads being uniform is key. I get mine at Shipwreck Beads (www.shipwreckbeads.com)

I get my warp at Weaving Works (http://www.weavingworks.com) 3/2 mercerized cotton makes a nice band and weaves up fast. 5/2 makes an even finer band, and weaves only slightly slower.

Web site on Akha fashion:

- http://tudtu.tripod.com/hillsty1.htm
- http://www.tienchiu.com/travels/thailand/the-akha-people/

Dragon Boats

Sturdy, un-corrugated cardboard is available at my local Ben Franklin, but can be found just as easily as the back of drawing tablets. In a pinch, even cold cereal boxes can be used!

The narrow ribbon I use in class comes from the local craft shop (Michael's, JoAnn, or Ben Franklin). Fancier ribbon is also available at specialty yarn stores. I got the shiny ribbon (*anny blatt* brand) used in the title picture of this chapter at the Weaving Works (http://www.weavingworks.com). It is made in France and is actually nylon tubing. The variegated form of this tubing makes an especially lovely Dragon Boat sachet.

Although not about this craft, YouTube offers many videos on the dragon boat races to enrich your class.

- http://www.youtube.com/watch?v=7_ann43lLMA
- http://www.youtube.com/watch?v=T1WQ90F4HlI

Acknowledgments

My first thanks go to the teachers and authors and artists who taught these skills to me. I honor you and treasure what you have given me.

My second thanks go to my classroom models: Vernye, Victoria, Matthew, Dean, Duncan, Sophie, Julie, Nicole, Emily, Alexandra, Anastasia, Olga, Hannah, Katherine, Summer, the other Sophie, Amy, Kimmie, Parker, Brooke, Casey, Melissa, Niamh, Callie Ann, Taryn, Dana, Sofia and Nicolas, Maxwell and Will, Emily and Marie and Christie, You are a joy to teach! Thanks to the many students, even from years ago, who returned to let me include photos of their lovely works.

Thanks also to my incredibly well-spoken proof readers, Barb, Shirley and Sara. Thanks to Leslie for keeping me on the straight-and-narrow, thanks to Shelly for all the memories, thanks to Cat Bordhi for having said 'Oh, write the *book*!'

Special thanks to my loving husband for the photography, the lay-out, the support and the patience. You are the best thing that ever happened to me.

Made in the USA
San Bernardino, CA
24 March 2015